THE ART OF
WHITTLING

THIS IS A CARLTON BOOK

Published in 2017 by Carlton Books Ltd
20 Mortimer Street
London W1T 3JW

10 9 8 7 6 5 4 3 2 1

Text © Carlton Books, 2017
Design © Carlton Books, 2017
Illustrations by Bold & Noble
Photographs by Niklas Karlsson

A CIP catalogue record for this book is available
from the British Library.

ISBN 978-1-78739-003-4

Printed in China

THE ART OF
WHITTLING

A WOODCARVER'S GUIDE TO
MAKING THINGS BY HAND

NIKLAS KARLSSON

CARLTON
BOOKS

CONTENTS

6   INTRODUCTION:
    A WHITTLER'S STORY

12 THE CARVED SURFACE

14 A WHITTLER'S TOOLS

16 Knives

20 Axes

26 Gouges

29 Spoon knives

32 Drawknives

34 Scorps and other
    special tools

36 Using a knife and axe safely

38 EQUIPMENT AND
    THE WORKSHOP

41 Keeping it simple

42 The chopping block

43 The shaving horse

45 Sharpening tools

50 Planes

56 WOOD

58 Understanding the grain

61 Identifying wood

63 Foraging and being
    self-sufficient

64 Types of wood

72 A WHITTLER'S SKILLS:
    THE PROJECTS

74 Splitting wood

77 Making a blank for a spatula

80 Carving a spatula

88 The burl and the guksi:
    carving a traditional
    Scandinavian drinking cup

96 Carving a spoon

108 A small shelf: some
    simple joinery

116 A whittled peg rack

126 Fågelsjö and the
    birch-bark box

144 Decorative woodcarving

150 Finishing

155 EPILOGUE:
    A NOTE ON SIMPLICITY

157 Resources

158 Index

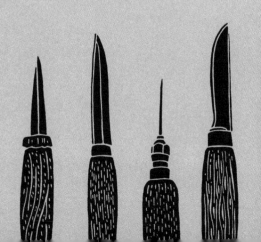

INTRODUCTION:
A WHITTLER'S STORY

I have been whittling for my whole life, really. It is a part of my family's culture. In 1822, my ancestors founded a settlement that is today the village of Grundsjö, in the south of Lapland. My grandfather made all that he needed from the wood around him. He crafted boats, horse-drawn vehicles, agricultural implements and hunting equipment. And he also made small things, such as knives, wooden cups and boxes from birch bark. I never met him; he died before I was born. My father comes from a family of 15 siblings and he is one of the youngest.

I grew up in Upplands-Väsby, a suburb of Stockholm, and I remember the light glinting through the opening in our garage door when my father was working in there at night. He taught me the basics of whittling during those nights in the garage, and I got to choose my own knife from a mail-order catalogue. It was a big folding knife for hunting. Not the best choice, I can say today. I vividly remember sitting under a giant spruce, deep in the forest, and unfolding that knife. I pulled the blade across my fingers and had to run all the way home, bleeding and crying. I used that knife to carve spears and bows for childhood games in the woods.

It was not until my early twenties that I started carving seriously. I travelled in the north of Sweden, and became taken with the Sami handicraft known as *duodji*. I ended up on a course with the Swedish crafter Ramon Persson, who has mastered everything, from sawing leather to interior carpentry. While I was making a wooden last for a leather case, Ramon commented that it looked as if I knew what I was doing. I remember thinking: "I do?" However, looking back, everything had already begun to fall into place. It felt as if we had made a pact, the wood and I. We had come to understand each other, as I sat beneath that spruce as a child and during those endless days up in the northern landscape where I spent most of my holidays.

After that course with Ramon, I decided to try to make my own knife and leather sheath. And that was when it hit me with full force – my love of wood. Up to this point, I had very few ambitions in life. Owning a Harley was the only one, really, and perhaps becoming a writer or songwriter. But now it felt as if I had something I wanted to do. I went to a folk high school in Vindeln, in Lapland, for two years and then studied Higher Craft Education at HV-school in Stockholm.

My father was happy about my choice of life, I think because I followed my heart. One time, he began to tell me the story of our family. I had wanted to hear about our Sami heritage for so long. He started by saying, "It was poor as hell..." Then he stopped. It was too difficult. And I have settled with that. He can take it to the grave with him. I'm fine with that now. Somehow the woodworking, carving and whittling take me back to those roots.

One of my most profound childhood memories was the time I visited a reindeer gathering. It was on a summer vacation, visiting my father's parental home. One evening, after dinner, we saw a helicopter flying low over Lake Bullersjön. My father, second oldest uncle and I were up at the old house on the far side of the mountain. My father asked my Uncle Rolf what the helicopter was doing there. "It is the Sami reindeer herders gathering their herd to move it," he said. "Let's go there."

We drove along the bad dirt road towards the lake in his Volvo, with the sounds of the helicopter and motorbikes, as well as the clicking of the reindeers' hooves and their bells in the forest, accompanying us.

Then we came across a man walking along the road. My uncle rolled down the window to ask him where the enclosure for gathering the herd was. The man instantly opened the door and got into the car, although he was soaking wet up to his thighs. "Just keep on straight ahead," he said. He told us he had been running along with the herd in the forest and morass, and that the helicopter and motorbikes were not enough when the reindeer approached the enclosure. He looked beat, but made a huge impression on me, of course. My dearest toy for the rest of that summer was a throwing loop.

1 & 2

A wooden cup and birch-bark boxes made by my father.

3

A Sami wooden kata at Fatmomakke, an old Sami meeting place.

1

2

Introduction: A Whittler's Story

3

Since then the Sami culture has had a place in my heart, I guess. But it wasn't until I was 25 years old that my Uncle Rolf told me that the settlers who had started the settlement and built the farm where my father was born, including my great-great-great grandfather, were actually Sami. But I also knew that our family didn't consider themselves to be Sami anymore. Because in the next sentence, as we chased an old, stray bull reindeer out of his tractor garage, my uncle said, "I hate reindeers and I hate Sami people."

Sami craftwork has a long tradition, and its foundation lies in natural materials; it is based on wood, birch bark, roots and the hides and antlers of reindeer. Textiles and some silver and other metals are also key elements in the Sami craft.

The essence of Sami craft is the utilitarian object as applied art, with function being central. The nomadic context and living with nature creates an organic artistic idiom. To me, there is even a sense in which the use and patina of the objects just add to this beauty. And that is what really inspires me about the Sami craft – and, I might add, traditional Swedish craft in the same context. Reindeer herding is truly a part of the Sami culture, and the craft associated with it is a part of the nomadic context. But there is also a mixture of cultures: those of the Sami and the settler, where Sami people, like my ancestors, became settlers to protect what was left of their pastureland, or because they didn't own a herd of reindeer. And it was a culture of wood.

THE CARVED SURFACE

All sanding equipment should be banned from a whittler's toolbox. There is no surface like the one made by a sharp knife (or any other cutting edge tool). After all, we live in the twenty-first century and have a blind trust in all things new. But there was a time, I have been told, in the history of the Scandinavian craft movement, when all advisors emphasized the importance of sanding. Oh, the time wasted!

The carved surface takes skill to achieve, but once you are able to make a clean, smooth carved surface as a finish on your whittlings, you do not need to spoil it with sandpaper. On a carved surface, the fibres have been cut straight off. The pores are open and there are no grains or dust to keep the finishing oil from sinking into the wood. There are no pushed-down fibres that can rise and make a spoon or spatula feel greasy and fuzzy when it is used.

The carved surface is outstanding for remaining hygienic and ageing with grace. This became really obvious when a young man sent me an email after ordering a cooking spoon to say that he and his girlfriend were going to clear out the plastic from their kitchen. The only thing that had kept them from doing so before was his girlfriend's dislike of the machine-made, wooden kitchen utensils available in supermarkets and design stores.

1

A well-used spoon made from birch, with a silky smooth patina. You can still see the tool marks made by the knife.

2

End-grain on a machine-produced spoon. The surface is sanded and the raised grain is clearly visible. To prevent a raised grain, this type of surface should be wet-sanded two or three times – a procedure that would probably multiply the cost of the spoon.

A WHITTLER'S TOOLS

16   KNIVES

20   AXES

26   GOUGES

29   SPOON KNIVES

32   DRAWKNIVES

34   SCORPS AND OTHER SPECIAL TOOLS

36   USING A KNIFE AND AXE SAFELY

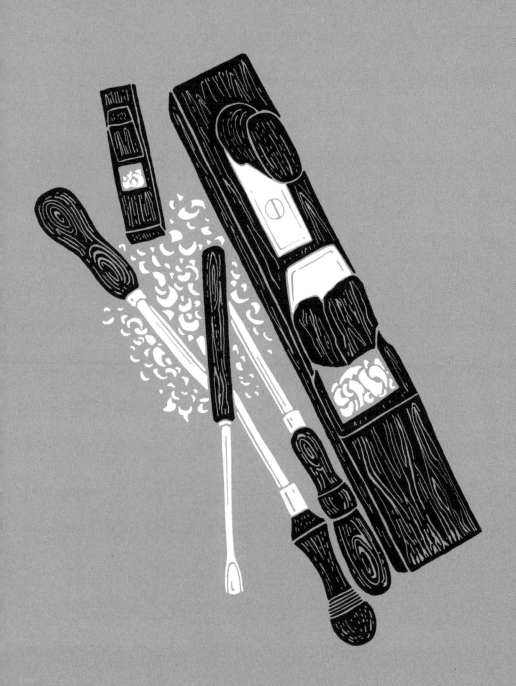

KNIVES

1

This knife belonged to my Uncle Pelle. It's a Sami knife, made by a friend of his. I got it for Christmas from my dad. It has a carbon-steel blade, and the sheath and handle are made from reindeer antlers.

2

From top to bottom: Three old Mora knives from different eras of the factory; a knife from J.A. Hellberg, Eskilstuna.

There is a huge variety of different knives available, but very few of them are useful for whittling. If you are new to whittling, you can be forgiven for thinking that any knife can be used to carve wood. But knives have all kinds of functions. Kitchen knives, for example, are mostly made for cutting straight down. You don't need any support from the bevel (the angle of the blade's cutting edge) when you cut, so kitchen knives have an extra bevel positioned right at the end of the blade, to make the edge more durable. Now I don't think anyone would use a kitchen knife to whittle a spoon, but the same type of extra bevel is found on most hunting knives (that is, the kinds of knives that people use as outdoor and bush-craft knives). You might be surprised to hear that these knives are not much good for whittling, either. The bevel is very important when you whittle. It provides the support you need to carve safely and with precision.

There are a few things to consider when looking for a whittling knife. I myself use the same kind of knife that the wooden-horse carvers of Nusnäs use to craft the traditional hand-painted Dala horses. A thin, smooth blade is more effective when it comes to carving distinct and curved shapes – on a spoon, for example.

My criteria for a good whittling blade are that it should be:

• *At least 8cm (3in) long.*

• *Laminated.*

• *Tapered.*

• *Not too thick (3–4mm/about ⅛in) is enough. On the other hand, if the blade is any thinner than that, the bevel will be too short.*

• *Pointy – with the blade being neither too broad nor too long.*

• *Preferably ready to use, with no need for sharpening.*

My recommendations

I prefer to use a laminated blade: this type of blade has a layer of hard carbon steel in the centre and softer steel containing less carbon on the sides. It is easier to sharpen and tends to have better qualities, because you can be sure it is specifically made for whittling. In contrast, full-steel blades and stainless-steel blades are more versatile and have a wider range of uses.

The knife that I use a lot is the Morakniv® woodcarving knife, specifically models 105 and 106 (these are more or less identical, but just have different handles). The model 120 is the same knife, but with a slightly shorter blade.

3

Two of my spoon-carving knives (top) and two knives used for carving traditional Dala horses (bottom). The blades have been well run down. The knives are model Slöjdkniv 105 by Morakniv®.

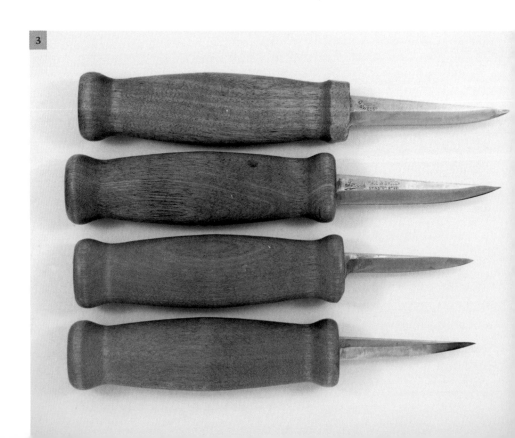

3

4

*Damascus blade
by Conny Persson,
with an extra bevel.*

5

*A blade for carving by
Bo Helgesson, without
an extra bevel.*

Knives

Above

Three broad axes. Axes like this are used
for hewing timber. From front to back:
An old axe from Wetterlings (length of
edge: 20cm/8in; weight: 1.9kg/4lb 3½oz);
a Gränsfors model 1900 (length of edge:
18cm/7in; weight: 1.6kg/3½lb); an old
Urafors axe (length of edge: 33cm/13in;
weight: 3.1kg/6lb 11½oz).

AXES

After the knife, the axe is the tool most associated with whittling. It is used for the rough and heavy work before you start the fine knife work.

As you start using an axe, you will find that it is useful for far more than just splitting a chunk of wood in half. You will discover that it is actually a precision tool that can be aimed exactly and make distinct cuts. It was a moment of awe for me to find myself, after four years of craft studies, in a small workshop in rural Slovakia watching a man cut a big bowl from aspen. He used a heavy axe with a long handle and roughly shaped the outside of the bowl with exact blows, while holding the blank with his foot. He then finished the surface with a drawknife. The inside was finished with a spectacular type of adze that I had only seen being used at that exact moment. No other tool was used for the inside of the bowl.

What makes an axe such a valuable complement to the knife is the weight behind the blade. It catapults through the wood and quickly reduces wood that isn't needed. When splitting wood, the axe is raised and the arms work as an extension of the handle. When carving with an axe, you only use your wrist to get momentum and the axe really just drops. So there is not necessarily that much effort behind each cut, but the force of the axe is high.

Left

The long, curved edge and the position of the handle on a carving axe make it easier to slice through wood at an angle; this makes the cuts more efficient. This is a Gränsfors large carving axe with an 11-cm (4-in) curved edge that weighs 1kg (2¼lb).

1

From left to right: An old axe (manufacturer unknown) with a striking resemblance to the Gränsfors carving axe (length of edge: 14cm/5½in; weight: 1.1 kg/2½lb); a Wetterlings carpenter's axe (length of edge: 10cm/4in, weight: 1.4 kg/3lb 3½oz); a Rönnqvist Töre, a hand-forged replica of an axe from the Viking Age (length of edge: 13cm/5in; weight: 700g/1½lb).

Carving with an axe

As with all carving, it is important that the axe blade cuts at a slight angle across the grain; for this reason, axes are shaped differently depending on their purpose. Today, the most common type of axe is the splitting axe. The edge of a splitting axe is quite short, because when you chop wood, you just want the axe to split the wood like a wedge. And the broader the edge, the more it tends to just bounce back with no impact on the wood.

Axes made for carving have a longer, more rounded edge, preferably with an upsweep towards the tip. To help further in making efficient sliding cuts, the handle is straight or curved backwards, so that your hand is placed "behind" the edge and not aligned with it.

The Gränsfors carving axe

Hand-forged axes have had a renaissance during the last few decades, after becoming virtually non-existent. A great deal of credit for this must go to the Gränsfors large carving axe. The last small manufacturers of axes ceased production in Sweden in the 1950s and 1960s. Up until then, timber was felled with axes, and one of the last axe-smiths in Hälsingland told me how they would be busy during the Christmas holidays, welding new steel into old axes, as well as making new axes, for the lumberjacks who started work in the forest in late winter/early spring.

In the early 1990s, master woodcarver and craft consultant Wille Sundqvist designed the

1

Sloyd axe for Gränsfors Bruk, an axe manufacturer in Hälsingland, Sweden. Gränsfors had reinvented traditional axes with wedged handles and bare iron heads, and in a way started the renaissance of hand-forged woodworking tools, along with Kaj Embretssen (custom-made knives and blades), Hans Karlsson and Svante Djärv (gouges, scorps and drawknives, etc.). Today there are a number of suppliers of well-made and traditional woodworking tools. Their numbers seem to be growing and their order books are full. But the Gränsfors large carving axe is something of a precursor of what we think an appropriate carving axe should look like. (Some people, however, consider it a bit too heavy, at least as an entry-level tool.) The handle is not too long and points upwards, while the edge is long and curved with an upsweep. It is designed for one-handed use and has quite a long beard, which allows the hand to have close contact with the axe-head when making precise cuts.

My recommendations

I would recommend the Gränsfors large carving axe as an all-round carving and whittling axe. If you feel it is a bit heavy, or you want to be sure you aren't about to choose an axe that's too heavy, then bear in mind that these axes have a large carving hatchet. A small carving hatchet is too light for carving, I think. The Hans Karlsson carving axe is a little lighter than the Gränsfors large carving axe. It's a good axe.

GOUGES

A gouge is not, perhaps, the first tool you should get when you start whittling. But if you want to progress a little further in woodworking, then a few gouges would be useful. To work with a gouge, you will also need a workbench of some kind to fix the piece of wood you are working on in place, since you have to hold the gouge with both hands.

The shape of the gouge depends on what it is going to be used for. Features that vary include the width of the blade, the curve of the edge and the shape of the shank, which can be bent or straight. Variations of these three features make the range of gouges almost endless. This is why a wood sculptor may have hundreds of different gouges. However, if you just want to carve a few differently shaped bowls, then you can manage with three to five tools.

Bent gouges are preferable for carving bowls where a straight shank can't reach. Straight, narrow gouges are very useful for different kinds of ornamentation and decorative carving.

1

A small gouge
used for carving
moulding.

2

From left to right:
A small gouge made
by Bo Helgesson;
four different
bent gouges (for
hollowing out
troughs and bowls)
by Hans Karlsson.

3

Straight gouges
from Pfeil.

4

A seat back that
has been decorated
with a small gouge.

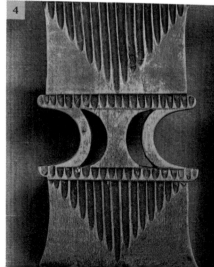

Above

*A bent gouge being
used in a large trough.*

My recommendations

I use Hans Karlsson's gouges, as I use
his other tools. So when it comes to
bent gouges for carving bowls and
troughs, I would recommend his.

Pfeil makes all kinds of chisels,
gouges and sculpting tools. The
finish is great and they are sharp
straight from the box.

A Whittler's Tools

SPOON KNIVES

A spoon knife is a fantastic tool. It enables you to work without a workbench and still make fantastic craft objects. I like the way in which you can take the tools and material with you to work outside or to a friend's place, or wherever you travel. If it weren't for the spoon knife, you would be stuck in a workshop with a workbench and gouges when you needed to hollow a spoon or wooden cup. Adding a few spoon knives to your toolkit opens up a whole range of new possibilities for your whittling.

Today, when I carve spoons, I manage to carve the bowls with just one spoon knife. When I first started, however, I needed two. Spoon knives are made with the edge either on the left or the right side of the blade. Whether left- or right-handed, you can use either type of spoon knife. The basic grip when using a spoon knife is to hold it in your right hand (if you are right-handed) with the edge pointing towards you and the tip pointing up. When you make a cut, you pull the knife towards your thumb; well, you actually pull it over your thumb. But I will talk more about this later. When you use a left-handed spoon knife, you hold it (even if you are right-handed) in your right hand with the tip pointing up. But the edge will now be facing away from you. So, the cut is made away from you, with the left-hand thumb pushing the knife and holding the piece of wood at the same time. It sounds difficult, but it will soon feel natural.

1

Spoon knives are not like the straight whittling knives found in ordinary hardware shops. And, for a long time, they were not at all common, even in a craft context. Instead, people favoured gouges, which were considered more of an artisan tool. A spoon knife is also more elaborate than an ordinary knife, on account of its bent shape and the fact that it is supposed to cut a concave surface. You may find that you don't get on well with certain spoon knives, and it is difficult to say just what makes a particular spoon knife useful or useless.

However, it is important that the bevel is not too short, so that the angle of the edge is not too big. A spoon knife should have a sharper angle on the edge than an ordinary knife.

My recommendations

Hans Karlsson's spoon knives are very good and can be ordered. I would recommend Bo Helgesson for all whittling tools (although his order book is often full because his tools are very popular).

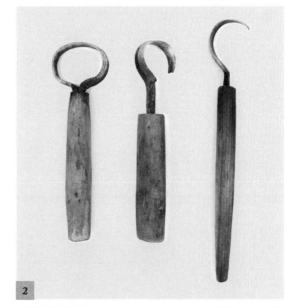

1

These are three of the knives I use most often. From left to right: A "left-handed" spoon knife by Hans Karlsson; a spoon knife by Svante Djärv; a spoon knife by Bo Helgesson. I bought the two knives on the right without handles, so that I could give them longer handles than the ones they usually come with. A longer handle on a spoon knife enables you to use more leverage and make greater use of both hands.

2

Three old tools: A carving loop on the left and two spoon knives. Old tools can be fascinating, but it takes some effort to make them functional. The spoon knives you can buy today are often more specialized and made of thinner material. Old tools might need to be thoroughly ground down in order to work well. The bevel needs to be long, to make a thin edge with a sharp angle.

3

The tool particularly associated with the Sami craft, duodji, is a carving loop with an attached strap. The strap is put around the neck to provide extra leverage, as well as to enable you to work with the muscles in your neck and back. The technique is very specialized and needs practice, even if you are already familiar with the spoon knife. It is a very powerful tool. And it is not difficult to imagine how useful it was for Sami craftsmen, who are well known for making wonderful objects out of birch burl.

From top to bottom: A spoon knife by Niklas Karlsson, for making big bowls; a spoon knife (with a neck strap) by Magnus Sundelin; a carving loop by Bo Helgesson.

DRAWKNIVES

1

A drawknife is held at an angle to the piece of wood, to give a slicing cut. I also start the cut on the far right of the blade and finish the cut on the left side. The slicing effect is made even more efficient in this way.

2

A drawknife made by Niklas Karlsson (top) and an old drawknife (below). Drawknives usually only have the bevel on one side. The flat side can be considered the underside and provides stability when you carve.

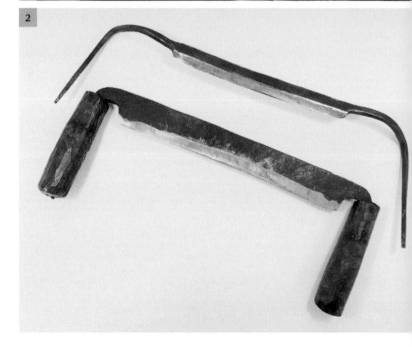

Drawknives have been used historically in many crafts, such as timber framing, and were common in medieval tool chests. But the tool is mostly associated with coopering, where it was used to make the staves for wooden casks. There are records from Dalecarlia, in Sweden, a place with a lively craft tradition, that describe how coopers went into the forest to get wood for coopering, but prepared the staves on location instead of returning home with the whole logs. They worked for days and made their beds with the shavings they produced.

A lot of whittlers make good use of the drawknife and the shaving horse, which is the best tool for holding the piece of wood in place while you work with a drawknife. However, a shaving horse is not a necessity. With a fairly small and light drawknife, a robust apron and perhaps a piece of board, you should be able to put the tool to good use.

Although a drawknife is pulled towards you, I consider it to be one of the safest tools you can use. Since you have both hands on the tool, you cannot cut your hand, as is the case when working with a carving knife. Neither are you at risk of stabbing your leg when working with a drawknife, provided that you use it properly. Although the long, sharp edge might feel hazardous, a drawknife is actually a very safe tool, as long as you handle it wisely when it's not in use.

My recommendations

Pfeil has a variety of drawknives. Hans Karlsson also makes one model of drawknife, a straight, short one.

SCORPS AND OTHER SPECIAL TOOLS

Some whittlers like to use the minimum number of tools. They want nothing more than a Mora knife, a Gränsfors wildlife hatchet and a few spoon knives so they can keep things simple – maybe it's a question of how much space they have at their disposal. Other whittlers are tool-nerds and collectors – for them, knowing as much as possible about the tools becomes a part of the whole whittling experience. Or perhaps they just enjoy fiddling with their precious tools and dreaming of all the things they could make with them.

I find tools fascinating, especially the primitive tools that have been found in the Sami and settler areas of northern Scandinavia. They can tell you so much about the conditions and way of life of these self-sufficient people. They had to live from, and with, nature – and abide by its laws.

A knife is often regarded as a plain, second-rate tool. In joiner colleges, for example, there are teachers who wouldn't even touch a knife, and if they found one being used in their class, it would be removed. But, in the self-sufficient context, a knife was a matter of life and death, and in a trained hand it is a universal tool. And in that context, most tools – like a knife – have the same simple but ingenious functionality.

You can use a scorp to cut the inside of large bowls. Historically, scorps were used for clean cutting the inside of wooden gutters. A scorp can also be used to cut a flat surface. It will leave a more pronounced and wavy surface than a hand plane, but that might be the intention. On the whole, I guess you could say that the simpler the tool, the more possibilities it will have.

1
A carved surface on a piece of maple board.

2
Three old scorps.

3
Two new scorps: A large scorp by Torsten Almén (left) and a small scorp by Svante Djärv (right). I made the handles myself.

1

2

3

My recommendations

Hans Karlsson has a traditional scorp which I would say is useful for troughs and gutters. Pfeil has a variety of tools – some are a combination of a carving loop and a scorp and others are a combination of a drawknife and a scorp.

USING A KNIFE AND AXE SAFELY

When I was a child, around eight or nine years old I should think, I got my own whittling knife. My father has told me since that he made sure I used it wisely before he let me out into the world with it. That is, my world in the woods and fields around the house. But, as I remember it, there were no such precautions.

Today, I sometimes get the feeling that most people regard knives and, of course, axes are included here, as too great a risk to consider using – even for grown-ups.

If you want to start whittling, there is a palpable risk that you will cut yourself. Small cuts and scratches are unavoidable. Maybe some will hurt, too, and need a little more than a sticky plaster. However, the injury should not get any more severe than that. To minimize risks of stabbing and hacking yourself, and getting badly injured, you need to behave carefully and cautiously.

It is easy to make hasty decisions, before you are comfortable with the tools and aware of the risks, especially at the start of your whittling journey. When you have gained some experience, your worst enemy is to be in a rush. I have noticed over the years that when you are used to working with an axe and a knife, your body learns a kind of risk assessment and you automatically anticipate the movements and actions of the tool. What happens if I use too much force on this piece of wood? What happens when a cut is performed like this? What if the piece is loosening from the vice? Nevertheless, I have a great respect for sharp tools, as I am quite fond of my fingers. Now I am more careful when handling tools. I usually cut myself when sharpening tools. Once, after sharpening a big timber axe, I stood with a whetstone in one hand and the axe in the other. When I put the stone away, I accidentally brushed my hand all the way across the edge of the axe, resulting in a deep stinging cut.

One of my birch-bark courses at Fågelsjö, where the old stable is used as a workshop.

Carving towards yourself

When you whittle you always hear: "You should only carve away from you." Well, one of the safest ways to carve is towards you. You just need to do it in a safe manner. When you pull a knife towards you, carving chips from a piece of wood, for example, you have to be absolutely sure that the blade will stop before it reaches any part of your body. Most knife grips that involve pulling the knife towards you have a built-in natural hindrance that actually makes it impossible for the knife to go too far. This you need to know.

In the step-by-step projects that follow later in the book, I go through the safety of the tools involved, the knife grips that I use, and how to perform them in a safe way.

However, here are a few basic safety tips to follow when using a knife:

- Sit down; you are in no hurry. This is often seen in classes – people who stand up to carve have poor control.

- Lock your arms close to your body.

- Put the knife down when you are not using it.

- Use sharp tools, because they behave in a more controlled way.

- Don't carve objects that are too small. This tip applies especially to those occasions when you are using an axe!

- Keep your work area tidy. Don't amass tools in piles and put away things that might make you stumble.

- Always fix broken tools. Don't let loose handles remain loose, for example.

EQUIPMENT AND THE WORKSHOP

41   KEEPING IT SIMPLE

42   THE CHOPPING BLOCK

43   THE SHAVING HORSE

45   SHARPENING TOOLS

50   PLANES

Above

To whittle, all you need are some basic tools and blanks made with an outdoor chopping block in your garden. I keep these in a basket and can have a productive day by the River Ljusnan, which is close to where I live. The day ends with some fly fishing, before I pick the kids up from school.

KEEPING IT SIMPLE

When I was studying craft, I remember that most of us wanted our own workshop on leaving school. Some of my friends even started their own businesses to achieve that dream. But they were perhaps a little hasty and found themselves in their long-awaited workshops without knowing what they were supposed to do. Their production was quite unconsidered and sprawling.

You can whittle without very much equipment. It mostly depends on your own demands. I have done my whittling in the hall, in the living room, in the basement storehouse. A friend of mine was caught whittling in bed, but I think that's the limit for me. After all, as a hobby, whittling produces chips and splinters, which can look a little messy strewn around an apartment. However, since most whittling is done without machines, there is no dust and the woodchips from carving can be swept up easily. In addition, it's my strong conviction that you can, if you wish, keep your whittling simple and still make it something you can do for a living. There are not very many examples of this scenario, but I think we will see more of them in years to come.

When I started making spoons, I sat in my kitchen in the mornings, lit a fire in the stove and turned on the radio. It was winter and, as I started working, the sun rose and the dark faded outside. Even though I had a workshop, the kitchen was where I wanted to work. When I had finished, I swept up the chips and went to collect the kids from school. The blanks were cut using a chopping block in the basement. Rough axe work can, of course, be a problem if you live in an apartment. When I was at college, we lived in an apartment in Stockholm and my dad used to hollow a big burl with an adze in the kitchen. I would think to myself, "This can't be good." But no one complained and he made a beautiful, big bowl that was later in an exhibition at the Museum of Architecture in Stockholm.

THE CHOPPING BLOCK

A chopping block is really useful. Without one you cannot rough-shape, split wood, etc., in a safe and practical way. Many chopping blocks are too low for carving with an axe, as you do when you axe out blanks. This is because most chopping blocks are only intended for chopping firewood. When you chop firewood, you want to reach the top of a standing log of wood in a convenient way. When you carve with an axe, the top of the chopping block is actually your workspace. So, it should be about the height of your crotch. Think of a countertop. If you happen to have a chopping block (for chopping wood) that is too low, you can raise it by adding three legs. The legs are easy to make out of thick branches that you drill in underneath the block. This also keeps down the weight of the chopping block and so is a good way of making it a little more portable. Fir is a good wood to use if you don't want your chopping block to be too heavy.

5

A chopping block elevated with legs is not as heavy as a traditional splitting block.

1

I start with a piece of birch. The diameter of the trunk is roughly 20cm (8in) and the height 30.5cm (12in). The legs are made from quarters of a small tree. Three legs provides the most stability if the ground is uneven. I use a wood drill bit with a diameter of 3cm (1¼in) and a hand brace to drill the holes. The wood should be dry. The holes are drilled quite deep – about 5–7.5cm (2–3in).

2

I estimate the angle at which the legs should be positioned. You want them to lean outwards to give stability to the chopping block. The long drill bit makes this easier. When the first leg is in place I can use it as a guide when I drill the next hole.

3

The principle when fitting the legs in the chopping block is the same as with the pegs for the peg rack (see pages 116–123). Before I hammer the legs in place I put a wedge in the top of the tenon. The wedge is driven in when it reaches the bottom of the hole, and makes the tenon expand. The length of the wedge should be about 2.5cm (1in). Carve the wedge safely from a longer piece

of wood and cut it to suitable length when it is finished. Carving wedges from a short piece of wood is a sure way to get hurt.

4

When all the legs are in place I put the chopping block on a flat surface and prop up the legs where needed until it stands straight. Now I can draw a line where the legs should be cut level, using a piece of wood or a folding rule between the pen and the floor.

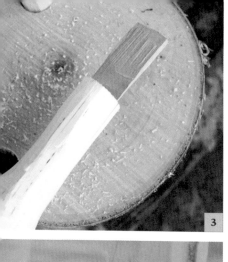

3

4 5

THE SHAVING HORSE

A shaving horse is mainly used for holding wood in place while you carve with a drawknife. So, if you are planning to get a drawknife, I recommend you own a shaving horse as well. A shaving horse is easy to build yourself and, because it also works as a bench, it is always useful to have. You have somewhere to sit, a place to saw and a means of clamping things.

I have made two shaving horses without thinking too much about the angles, ergonomics or technology. The construction is very basic; what is important is that you can put as much force on the pedal as possible. The more leverage you can get from the pedal to the clamp, the steadier the grip. Therefore, it is important that the pedal is positioned in front of the clamp, so that just by putting the weight of your leg and foot on the pedal, there is a force/pressure on the clamp, to hold the wood in place.

Below

My shaving horse. The head is extra long, so the gap will fit a large trough.

SHARPENING TOOLS

Without sharp tools, your efforts will be wasted and whittling won't be at all rewarding. So how do you sharpen your tools? Sharpening is a two-step process. The first step is to use a grinding stone to get the appropriate set-up of the bevel and to shape the edge. The second step is to polish the metal using whetstones, to make the edge sharp.

Most people have a basic knowledge of the second step, but few know what the first step involves. But if you think that you can sharpen a knife just by using whetstones, then you will find it very hard, once the blade has worn down a little, to get a really sharp tool.

Here I demonstrate what is, in my opinion, the best way to get a good bevel and a sharp edge on a whittling knife. I prefer to use water-cooled grinding stones to grind the knife and also to use water on the whetstones. There are other types of whetstones; I'm thinking here of diamond whetstones, which are very hard and mostly used for sharpening kitchen knives.

Grinding stones

The grinding stones I use are water-cooled stones. Some people prefer other methods of sharpening, but I don't think these are a good choice. Water-cooled grinding stones give the slightly concave bevel you want, without the risk of burning the edge. If you already have a bench grinder and want to use that, then you have to be sure not to burn the edge of the blade. If the blade gets too hot, the tempering of the steel will go away and the edge will lose its strength. Have a bowl of water close to hand and cool the blade often. But, aside from this, a bench grinder is also very small. As a result, the bevel will be too concave and the edge of the blade will get thin and fragile. It is also difficult to achieve controlled ergonomics. With a belt sander, you have the same problem with burning the blade. A belt sander also has the disadvantage that the bevel is easily rounded, which makes the honing harder.

When you think of a water-cooled grinding stone, it is easy to imagine a big, heavy stone with a foot pedal or crank – the kind your grandfather might have had by the barn wall – but this is not the case. There are small, portable grinding stones on the market, which are really easy to move around and to put away when not in use. Tomek is perhaps the best-known brand. This works really well, but is something of a professional machine. Fortunately, you can find budget alternatives that are just as good.

Grinding the blade

The grinding of a blade is not done that often. It is not necessary until the blade has been so run down that it is hard to get a sharp edge using the whetstones, or when the blade/edge has been really damaged. New tools need to be sharpened, too, as you can't be sure that they have useful edges straight from the box.

1

Grinding your knife on a water-cooled grinding stone is all about practice and making your hands do what your mind has set itself to do. This is why it is good to have a method that you repeat in the same way each time. My method is to start to grind at the base of the blade and move to the tip, and then lift the blade and repeat. If you go back and forth too much, you risk losing control of the angle.

- Stand in front of the stone, with the stone rotating towards you. Put one foot forwards and one foot back, so that you are standing with stability.

- Hold the knife in one hand and use the other hand to support the blade on its back side with your fingers. Lock your arms to your body.

- Lower the blade onto the stone, but without the edge touching it; in other words, lay it down on the back, flat side of the blade. Don't press on the blade.

- Tip the edge forwards until the whole bevel rests on the stone. Listen to the sound: when the whole bevel is supported by the stone, the sound usually goes from quite a coarse to a softer scraping sound. Watch the water as well: when the water flows over the edge, it is touching the stone. Don't tip the blade forwards too much, or it can grab.

- Put a little pressure on the blade. Hold it steady and try to memorize the angle of your body.

- Lift the blade and control the grinding marks.

2

You can easily check if you've got the angle right controlling how far the stone has reached on the bevel: if the grinding marks are just at the tip of the edge, you have pressed on the edge too much; if the marks are just on the back of the bevel, then you need to press on the edge more. I hold the handle of the knife so that I can adjust the pressure on the edge with my thumb and index finger. The index finger is pressing the edge down/forwards, and the thumb is holding back (see Step 1).

Repeat the testing, if necessary. It is easier to get the angle right at the base of the blade. Once you think you have the angle right, put a little more pressure on the knife, but not too much. Slowly move the knife over the stone until you reach the tip of the blade. When you reach the bend of the tip, pull the handle back slightly, so that the edge is held at 90 degrees to the stone at all times.

Equipment and the Workshop

3

Lift the blade and control the grinding marks. Repeat the motion from the base to the tip until the whole bevel is ground.

4

Grind the other side of the blade. Most people find that one side of the blade is easier to grind than the other (that is, when holding the knife in their preferred hand). To grind the other side, you need to hold the knife in the "wrong" hand. It is the only way, I'm afraid.

Once both sides have been ground and the stone has really reached out across the whole edge/bevel, a raw edge is formed on the sharp edge. It is produced by waste metal being pushed up by the stone. The raw edge is a sign that there is no blunt part of the edge left and, therefore, that honing can begin. You can't always see the raw edge with the naked eye, but it can be felt by gently running your finger down the side of the blade and over the edge.

Whetstones

Whetstones have different grain sizes or grit. Ceramic whetstones have an exact grit, which is produced artificially by mixing a ceramic material with an abrasive. Natural whetstones are cut and sourced from a natural rock with the right qualities for sharpening tools. This means that natural whetstones are not as exact but, in my experience, they are often somewhere in between soft and hard.

I was once sitting in an exhibition demonstrating whittling and, as I was sharpening my knife with my ceramic whetstones, an old man came up to me. He asked me what stones I used and I showed him my ceramic whetstones. He chuckled a little when I told him how much they cost, and told me that I should use a whetstone from Los, a small place close to the area where I live, and a strap. And he was right; it worked really well. Some whittlers say that a strap will make the edge rounded, and this is probably true, but so will a whetstone over time and we still use them. I think it's a matter of how dogmatic you want to be.

So, sometimes I use ceramic whetstones and sometimes I use natural stones. Ceramic stones are fine for making a final edge. With natural stones, I finish the edge with a strap. The carvers who make the traditional painted Dala horses have a nice little trick of polishing their blades on newspaper. The printing ink on the newspaper contains silicon, which polishes the blade to a really fine edge.

1

A knife, three whetstones and a strap. The stones in the middle are, from left to right: A red ceramic "Japanese" whetstone (grit 1,000); a natural stone from Gotland (Sweden's largest island); half of a yellow "Japanese" whetstone (grit 8,000).

2

When the honing is done, and if you managed to get a good set-up of the bevel on the grinding stone, you will see that the whetstones have only polished the edge and the back of the bevel. This is due to the fact that the bevel is slightly concave, which is created by the grinding stone.

Sharpening the edge

I start honing with a low-grit whetstone, that is, grit 1,000. When the blade has just been ground, the raw edge is quite prominent and needs to be removed. Because of this, I frequently switch sides. I hone one side of the blade briefly, using just a few strokes of the whetstone, and then the other side. This is not as important when the blade has been honed a few times, as then you can do one side at a time.

Hold the knife steady and rest it with the whole bevel on the stone. Don't tip up the point of the edge, because this will make the edge round. Soak the stone with plenty of water while you hone. I hold the knife still and move the stone in circles, holding it vertically in front of me. When I shift sides, I change the grip on the knife. Other people like to lay the whetstone down in front of them and move the knife in circles on it. Whichever method you choose will work, as long as the bevel is flat on the stone and not wiggling back and forth.

There is no need to overdo the honing when the blade is just ground, because you will destroy the nice set-up of the bevel. But the raw edge needs to be taken away.

- Switch to a finer grit; I go from 1,000 to 8,000. Polish the blade with the whole bevel resting on the stone. I continue to switch sides frequently, to ensure I take away the remaining raw edge.

- If you want a razor-sharp edge, you can strop the edge. You can make your own strop by gluing a piece of leather to a straight piece of wood. Apply some kind of polish (such as Autosol or Dialux) to the leather. The wood gives stability to the leather strap, which prevents rounding of the edge. Push the blade, with the bevel flat down and the edge pointing back, across the leather strap.

The ceramic whetstones can be replaced with a natural stone and combined with a strop.

PLANES

Planes might be associated with bench joinery and men with beards, but they have their place in whittling as a means to help smooth rough surfaces and make small boards out of fresh wood. They are also great to use when you want to reclaim old boards. All you need to do is give your boards a light touch with a sharp smoothing plane and they are as good as new. It is a special kind of magic.

Flattening rough wood to create a board

With straight-grained wood that splits nicely, it isn't too much of a leap to carve your own boards to make breadboards, seats, etc. For these items, you will need a few hand planes.

1

From left to right: A smoothing plane (length: 23cm/9in); a jointer plane (length: 76cm/30in); a jack plane (length: 30cm/12in).

Start by flattening a reference face on one side. When you have a split piece of wood, the first planing can be quite rough. Use a plane with a curved blade, as it removes large quantities of wood. At this point, you don't have to think too much about the surface being smooth. Just try to make the face of the board reasonably flat.

2

Work diagonally across the board. Remove axe marks and high points until you have a rough, but flat, surface.

3

Take big chips with a curved blade to remove material quickly.

4

Once you have removed the axe marks and high points, use a big jointer plane to flatten the board. A longer plane won't follow the curves and slumps, and is a sure way of only removing the high points. If you hold the plane diagonally to the wood, the blade will cut better. Hold the plane at an angle, while moving it in the direction of the grain.

3

4

5

Aim down the board and see if the plane twists. Hold a try-square, or the edge of the plane, across the board to discover low points.

6

Smooth the board with a fine-tuned smoothing plane. If the grain breaks, change the direction of the planing. It is not unusual for the grain to run in one direction on one side of the pith and the other way on the other side.

7

Put the board on a flat surface, with the reference side facing down. Find the lowest point and scribe around the edge with a distance. You can also use a scribe tool or marking gouge to do this. (If you don't want to retain as much as possible of the board's thickness, then any measure can be used, of course.)

8

Place the board between the bench dogs. Here, I started by making a facet down to the line on both sides, which meant I "only" had to remove the high ridge left in the middle and the board was done. As for the reference side, I started by using a jack plane with a curved blade and removed most of the material, axe marks and chippings made by the splitting. I switched to a long jointer plane and then finished the surface with a smoothing plane. I also made minor adjustments with the smoothing plane where necessary.

9

One board ready and one board split and axed. This finished board is made from outdoor fresh wood. This means it will bend during the drying process and so will probably have to be adjusted one more time.

Wooden planes

Planes are a vast subject, involving many specialized types with a wide range of uses. I will only discuss the most common features of planes, the issues you may encounter when attempting slightly larger projects in your whittling, and what to do when you find yourself owning one or two old or new planes and want to start using them.

Working with planes is very much about setting them up to work well. And it also has a great deal to do with good ergonomics.

Wooden planes are slightly more demanding on the user; there are more things to keep track of and you have to be light with your hand, as each individual plane can have its own little whims. So let's start with those.

1

The parts of a wooden plane, from left to right: The body or stock; the blade; the cap iron; and the wedge. The opening for the blade is called the mouth and the cheeks hold the wedge in place.

- The first thing to check is, of course, the blade. If you have read the chapter on sharpening and learnt how to sharpen a knife (see page 49), you will be able to manage a plane. The blade of an ordinary plane is easy to sharpen. The thing to know is that you should not make the blade absolutely straight, but a little curved. A completely straight blade will leave traces in the face of the board from its sharp corners.

- Next, it is very important to check what shape the cap iron is in. The cap iron is the piece of metal that sits on top of the blade and is used to break the chips the blade is cutting and to prevent tear-out in the board. The cap iron needs to be tight against the blade so that no chips can get stuck between the blade and the cap iron. If this happens, the woodchips will jam in the mouth of the plane. If there is a gap between the cap iron and the blade, it is usually the cap iron that needs adjusting.

2

The shavings are curled against the cap iron or chip breaker. It should be tight against the blade and nicely polished and smooth. For fewer tear-outs and for finer shavings, the cap iron should be positioned close to the cutting edge of the blade.

- On wooden planes the blade and cap iron are held in place by a wedge. Sometimes chips get stuck in the extending legs of the wedge. In these cases, they can be shortened.

- On old wooden planes the sole, or base, might be uneven. To even out the sole, put a long strip of sandpaper on a completely flat surface. The sandpaper must be longer than the plane and at least as wide. Glue or tape it to the surface and, with a firm motion, grind down the sole of the plane until it is flat.

Setting the blade depth

You can adjust the depth of the blade on a wooden plane simply by striking the back of the blade with a hammer or mallet. To loosen the blade, you strike the back of the plane, or on the top of the body for some planes, just in front of the blade, where there is usually a button made of wood or metal so that the body of the plane itself will not be damaged.

I usually put the blade in so that it won't take anything at all and fasten it with the wedge. Then I gently tap the blade with a mallet and try the plane on a piece of wood. When the blade is taking shavings as thick as I would like, I fasten the wedge once more. It is a good idea always to use the same tool when adjusting the

blade. That way, you will always get the same result.

Metal planes

A metal plane is in many ways easier to use than a wooden plane. The blade depth is adjusted with a screw that you can manage with two fingers, so it can be adjusted on the go. The blade is easier to remove and the sole is cast, so you never need to adjust the sole and the mouth.

3

A metal plane with its iron body and the screw for adjusting the blade depth; instead of a wedge, the blade and cap iron are held in place with a lever cap. The blade can also be adjusted sideways, using the lever above the depth-adjustment screw.

4

A hand-planed surface – the marks from the hand plane give a piece life and structure.

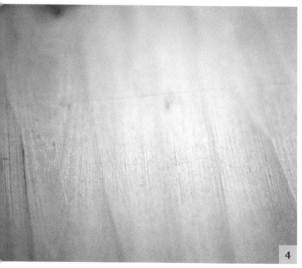

WOOD

58   **UNDERSTANDING THE GRAIN**

61   **IDENTIFYING WOOD**

63   **FORAGING AND BEING SELF-SUFFICIENT**

64   **TYPES OF WOOD**

UNDERSTANDING THE GRAIN

Everyone who starts whittling gets the feeling sooner or later that the wood is working against him or her. The surface just won't smooth, chips break off where they aren't supposed to, and the knife gets snared and stuck. Wood has its own natural laws, although you will eventually learn how to master the grain. However, it might be useful to start with a few ground rules.

Perhaps you have heard people talking about carving with the grain or against the grain?

Wood is, in fact, a living material. So, it is basically a plant. And, like most plants, it grows in layers, from the inside and out, putting one layer after the next. This is why trees have growth rings. When you make a board out of a tree, the fibres run along the board and there is end-grain at both ends where the long fibres running along the tree stem have been cut off.

As long as you peel off one layer at a time, the wood will follow, but when you want to carve complex shapes such as curves and cavities in the wood, you will discover that you cannot keep carving without thought. You have to be aware of when the knife goes up against the direction of the grain and then change the direction of the knife. That is why you see people constantly turning their piece of wood and changing their grip as they carve.

There is an expression that you should carve downhill and not uphill. And it is a quite good expression if you picture the layers in the wood at the same time – you have to slide down the layers with your knife.

IDENTIFYING WOOD

I was listening to a radio programme one day – I don't remember what it was about – but a man called in during a discussion on birds. The man only knew about three kinds of birds: forest birds, seabirds and ptarmigan. I can relate to that because, although I work with wood, come across different qualities of wood and handle a lot of wood, I am only an expert within a narrow field. I don't know about a lot of different kinds of wood and I am really lousy at distinguishing between different types of trees. But my experience grows every time I come across a new type of wood. I haven't worked with fruit trees very much, but I got a piece of apple tree last summer and carved a few nice spoons. The thing about whittling is that you quickly get a feeling for the wood material; you value things that you cannot see, but feel. The apple wood was quite hard, kind of winding, and difficult to split. Overall it was not the type of wood you would want to work with hand tools if you were not trained. But the grain is spectacular, with deep colours. When whittling, you size up the wood you are in contact with and create your own database of experience.

The river Ljusnan.

2

My son and a big
birch burl I found.

My father finds a big sallow
root burl. These burls grow
partly underground, in
the transition between the
root and the stem, and are
sometimes covered with
small sprouts.

FORAGING AND BEING SELF-SUFFICIENT

It seems that my dad gives me most of my wood for whittling. Every time he visits, he has a load of birch with him. And I prefer to use fresh wood; in other words, I don't have to make the time and effort to dry it. For me, buying my wood is not an option, except for when I need sawn timber. In fact, taking my own material is what I seem to like most about the whole whittling process. I have lots of projects waiting to be finished, and when I think about why this is, I have to face the fact that I feel much more when starting something new. It's that excitement you get when you open up a new piece of wood, smell it, feel it, and see its opportunities. When it is dried and almost finished and, for me, saved and cared for, I like to find my next piece of wood and start the journey again.

TYPES OF WOOD

Every piece of wood is unique; one tree can be straight and easy to split, while for some reason another tree is twisted and full of cross-grain. This has to do with the conditions under which the tree has grown, but it is not that easy to see which is straight and which is twisted. However, the straighter and more even the stem, the more likely it is that the grain is good.

Trees are divided into deciduous and coniferous. The deciduous trees have leaves and the coniferous trees have needles. The coniferous trees, such as pine and fir, contain resin that protects the trees. Pine in particular is used for building houses, because of its natural resin that prevents decay.

The deciduous trees are divided into hardwood and softwood. The hardwood are trees such as oak, beech and maple. These trees may be possible to work when they are fresh, but once dried it is very hard to process the wood with handtools. They are prevalent in joinery and carpentry, in which machines are used.

Birch, aspen and alder all belong to the softwoods. These woods are not considered very valuable. To a whittler, that can be an opportunity. Good wood for whittling is not hard to find, as they are considered weeds to some people; small trees are just left on the ground when woodlands are thinned out. Most softwoods split easily and can be processed with handtools, even after they are dried.

Always ask the landowner if you can take trees, even if they are on the ground.

Fresh/green wood

The process of taking your own wood for whittling is a very special one. Not that it is complicated in any way – it is quite the opposite, in fact – but you need to know what happens when wood dries. The process for me goes something like this:

When I get the material, I make sure it is kept outside, but away from the sun when it dries. I can only keep fresh wood for a certain length of time. In the winter, it is quite safe, but in the summer it is in danger of getting drying cracks and also rotting.

If you have a big supply of fresh wood and can keep it in a place where it won't rot, it will eventually dry, and then you have dry wood instead, which is good. To prevent wood from getting too many drying cracks, I split it into smaller pieces. When I acquire a lot of wood at the same time – perhaps because someone has asked me if I would like a whole tree that they've cut down – I cut the stem into logs, about 1m (3ft) in length. Then I split them through the pith and maybe also once or twice more into thinner pieces/slabs. The slabs are kept outside under a roof or in a fairly cold place. Once they have dried to outdoor dryness, I can either keep them that way or continue to dry them indoors.

Birch (*Betula*)

In the north of Sweden we have one tree that is prominent in whittling: birch. Birch is the wood that people use for firewood – it is very common, but it is very useful, too. The birch is not a hardwood, but it is not too soft either. It is really quite perfectly balanced when it comes to hardness. Birch is easy to work with hand tools compared with harder woods, but it doesn't feel as if you are compromising on the durability or quality of the woodware.

Silver birch (*Betula pendula*) and downy birch (*Betula pubescens*) are both good for whittling, but I think the downy birch is a little less cross-grained and easier to split. For me, birch is the number one wood for making spoons and other kitchen utensils. The blanks can be quite roughly shaped when they are put to dry, because dry birch is still manageable when cutting. Birch makes nice troughs and bowls, too. The wood also doesn't emit flavours that will contaminate food.

1

Long and straight downy birch stems with smooth bark.

2

Curly birch (Betula pendula var. carelica) is a rare type of birch with a recognizable grain. Since it is a genetic variation, it can be grown at home, but it is also found in the wild. The stem is knobbly and knotted, and the bark is cracked, almost leaving the wood bare.

3

Curly birch wood is very hard to carve, and is mostly used to make the handles of knives.

Types of Wood

1

Pine tree.

2

A sculpture by Per Nilsson Öst, made from an old pine tree that died while standing. Per created his sculptures with an axe.

3

A dead pine that is still standing.

4

Reclaimed pine, processed with a broad axe.

Aspen (*Populus tremula*)

I gladly use aspen for bowls and troughs. It grows big and is easily split without a cross-grain. It is one of the softer woods in Sweden, although it can feel as if you have picked a wood that is too soft when you make things such as spoons and spatulas. But it is easy to carve and great for learning.

Pine (*Pinus sylvestris*)

Pine is a highly regarded wood in carpentry and joinery. It is better to work dry than fresh on account of the resin, which is not pleasant when you get it on your hands and clothes. The contrast between the springwood and the summerwood in pine and other conifers also makes these woods difficult to carve, especially when fresh. The knife will hop through the wood.

Pine is very good to plane and works well for making furniture, and so on. The wood is good for splitting boards and slabs. Pine is maybe the best wood to recycle. It is frequently used in old buildings for floors, panels, ceilings and beams. Recycled pine is beautiful to work with. The variation in the annual rings seems to be evened out and it gets better with age. The old beams and logs from timber houses can be incredibly densely grown and have a beautiful red colour. In contrast with fresh pine, this wood is very nice to carve if you are lucky enough to find some. The reputable wood-artist Per Nilsson Öst, from Järvsö, in Sweden, worked with old "silver" pines; these are pines that have died while still standing. Because of the high content of resin in the wood, they can stand for hundreds of years in the forest. After that they fall and can lie as dead wood for hundreds of years. These pines are now protected, but the wood is similar to that of the recycled logs from buildings. It is a very homogeneous and enjoyable wood to carve. Plus, it may be a few hundred years old, which makes it a bit grand.

Softwoods

I will mention some of the softwoods that are good for whittling only briefly. For a beginner at whittling, softwood in itself can be enough of a challenge.

The wood from lime trees (*Tilia cordata*) is one of the softest woods you can work with. It is mostly used for sculpting and carving figures, but it doesn't grow very far north in Sweden, so isn't used much in this part of the country.

Alder (*Alnus glutinosa* and *Alnus incana*) and sallow (*Salix caprea*, a type of willow also known as goat willow) are both good softwoods for whittling. Sallow will split very cleanly and nicely. Both of these woods turn a red/orange colour when they oxidize, but the wood is pale when dried and carved clean.

Hardwoods

Ash (*Fraxinus excelsior*) and maple (*Acer platanoides*) are two beautiful hardwoods that I use frequently. Once dried, they are very hard to carve, so when I carve spoons from maple or ash, I carve them as close to being finished as possible before I dry them. Both of these woods are easy to split. I don't recommend carving bowls from ash or maple. They are better suited to planing and carpentry work, because it is difficult to work with a gouge or a scorp in hardwood.

1

Ash

2

Maple

3

Apple wood (Malus domestica)

A WHITTLER'S SKILLS: THE PROJECTS

74   SPLITTING WOOD

77   MAKING A BLANK FOR A SPATULA

80   CARVING A SPATULA

88   THE BURL AND THE GUKSI:
     CARVING A TRADITIONAL SCANDINAVIAN
     DRINKING CUP

96   CARVING A SPOON

108 A SMALL SHELF: SOME SIMPLE JOINERY

116 A WHITTLED PEG RACK

126 FÅGELSJÖ AND THE BIRCH-BARK BOX

144 DECORATIVE WOODCARVING

150 FINISHING

SPLITTING WOOD

For many people, whittling is associated with sore hands and hard, unrewarding work, just to achieve the slightest impact. That can all change once you understand how to split wood and break it down into blanks. It is the most basic technique in whittling and a very important one. A good piece of wood with which to start your whittling is a thin slice of a fairly small tree, preferably a soft, deciduous wood such as birch, alder or aspen.

There is one crucial rule to follow when you split wood: in order to get the wood to split straight, you have to split it down the middle of the mass. You cannot split one small piece of wood from a bigger piece and expect it to split straight. You have to split the mass in half and then in half again, and so on, until you get the size you want. And you should always start by splitting the wood through the pith (that is, the centre of the tree).

1

First, cut off a piece of stem (by making two crosscuts), so that it is about the size of a log of firewood.

2

Place the piece of wood on a chopping block and position an axe or froe straight across the pith.

3

Take a heavy wooden mallet and, with one hand holding the axe and the other holding the mallet, split the wood in half. I try to hold the blade of the axe in line with my feet, so that if the wood splits very easily, the axe won't catapult through the wood and towards my legs.

Splitting Wood

4

Now that you have two halves, you will need to split each of the halves into a quarter. To make a blank, you want to split one of the halves into a thinner piece, but keep the width. This is known as splitting the wood tangentially. You can also split the wood radially, as you would slice a cake.

5

When you split half of a log tangentially, cut closer to the pith than to the bark. The quarters should not be symmetrical, so the wider part will be a little thinner instead.

6

If the second split goes well, you will have two thin pieces of wood, including one with the bark still on it. You want the one with a split surface on both sides.

MAKING A BLANK FOR A SPATULA

With a thin piece of wood, like the one made by splitting the wood into quarters (see page 76), there are all kinds of possibilities for whittling useful things. And, depending on what you want to create, you can use an axe to take away even more material before you start with the knife work. The rough shape you get from the axing is called a blank. In this case, we are making a blank for a spatula, which is a very useful kitchen utensil.

My friend Stefan Olsson, who is a great troubadour but also a dedicated cooking enthusiast, once said that his wooden spatula (which he bought from me), along with his de Buyer carbon-steel frying pan, is his favourite utensil in the kitchen. So, making a utensil that will become indispensable to your cooking is perhaps something to aspire to.

A spatula can be made in many different ways. At its most basic, it is not too complicated to carve. The one shown in this project has no bent shapes and no curve in the blade, so the carving is just straight along the grains.

1

First, take down the material to shape the handle of your spatula. I like to make small cuts in order to break the fibres into smaller pieces. If you begin the cut where you want the handle to start, there will be a whole fibre running all the way down, holding the wood that you want to cut off.

2

Now cut the fibre into small lengths, which will make it easier to break off the wood.

3

Cut away material from where the blade of the spatula is supposed to start down to the top of the handle. The sides of the handle do not need to be parallel at this point; there can be more material towards the blade, but carve the top down to about the finished size – let's say 15mm (⅝in).

4

The dimensions of the blade can also be adjusted at this stage. Carve down the sides of the blank so that the blade isn't too wide. If you have a short blade on the knife, then the blade on a spatula that is too wide can be hard to carve. In this case, the blade on the roughed-out spatula measured 7cm (3in) across. You can easily adjust the width of the blade, of course, once you start carving with the knife.

5

The finishing axe work for the handle is made from the top and down towards the blade. This is a very risky cut that can spoil the blade if you cut too far. You can prevent this from happening by using a saw instead of the axe to make the crosscut – just use the saw to make a cut straight down.

A Whittler's Skills: The Projects

First, make a crosscut from the side, holding the blank horizontal on the chopping block. To make the axe cut into the wood, hold it at a slight angle. Be careful not to slant the axe too much, though, as you run the risk of it coming towards your hand if the cut slips.

6

When you have made crosscuts on both sides of the handle, carve with great caution from halfway up the handle down towards the blade. Keep the hand holding the blank as far away from the axe as possible, to ensure your thumb doesn't pop out onto the side you're carving. Make sure the cut stops half an inch before the blade and on the outer side of where the crosscut stops. Then break off the remaining fibres, so that you can finish the cut with a breaking movement of the axe, twisting the axe's head out a little from the handle of the spatula.

Repeat the crosscuts on both sides of the handle until it is the right size

where it enters the blade. Smooth and clean up the handle with a few gentle cuts.

7

Thin out the blade by taking some material from the front. The tip of the blade shouldn't measure more than 6–8mm (¼–⁵/₁₆in) or so when you have finished.

8

Thin out the handle on the back, to create a slight crank on the spatula. It is important you don't have the feeling when holding the finished spatula that the blade is "tipping down". By thinning out the handle from the back, you are more likely to get the feeling that the blade is pointing up a little instead, which will make the cooking experience more pleasant.

Since this blank was made from birch, it was dried before carving. To carve a dry hardwood that was this roughly shaped would not be an easy job.

Making a Blank for a Spatula

CARVING A SPATULA

Carving a spatula is a great way to get the basics of whittling. It is quite a safe object for a beginner to make since it is mostly straight carving and it is fairly easy to understand the direction of the grain. But what is even greater is that as simple as it may be, you will really enjoy it when you understand how useful it is. I love the spatula that I use every day when I am cooking. It is a prototype, really, for a spatula that I made in collaboration with the UNESCO World Heritage Centre in Järvsö to sell in their shop. But the prototype turned out to be the best. I find myself sometimes studying the details that I like about that particular spatula. Perfecting simplicity can be the hardest thing.

1

1 & 2

First, clean up and shape the back of the blade with a knife. I mostly take away material at the tip of the spatula. It gets a little crank upwards in this way. The knife grip I use here is the most basic one – the one that most people associate with whittling. Hold the knife with the blade pointing away from you and, with the bevel resting firmly on the wood, push the knife forwards. This grip is simple enough to understand, you might think, but there are ways to make it really controlled and powerful, as follows:

- Keep the arm holding the knife straight. Push the knife forwards with your shoulder rather than using the muscles in your arm. It should feel a little as if you are pushing the knife down towards the floor.

- Keep the hand holding the knife pressed firmly against the corresponding leg (either left or right).

- Pull the piece of wood towards you slightly, with your hand and forearm locked close to your body, while you push the knife away from you. Make the cut by moving both of your hands, but ensure that neither of these movements is very wide.

- Watch out for the point of the knife. Keep your knees wide apart and your body leaning forwards to get some space between your legs and the knife.

Some people prefer to keep their legs together when they use this grip (especially if they are teaching). Instead, they turn their body so that the knife is on the outside of the opposing leg and, in so doing, make the grip even safer; the point of the knife is really directed into thin air. I have never practised this technique myself, but it might be an option if you are new to whittling. In the long run, however, I think your back feels better if it is kept straight.

3

I like to create a distinct curve to mark the transition between the handle and the blade. This knife grip allows you to twist the blade effectively as you push it forwards. The hand holding the knife is just controlling the movement and twisting the knife, while the hand holding the piece of wood is also pushing the knife. You should prepare the grip like this:

- Grab the blank by clenching it with just four fingers, leaving your thumb free and pointing up towards your face. Rest the hand supporting the piece of wood in your lap.

- Hold the knife so that the edge is pointing away from you, and then put the blade in position for the cut.

- Put the thumb (of the hand holding the piece of wood) on top of the blade and push the knife down/forwards.

As you push the knife forwards, twist the blade from going straight into the wood until it goes out of the wood entirely. Make the movement quite swift and gentle. Take small pieces of wood, but repeatedly, and let the curve develop. This grip won't let you reach very far – one or two inches at the most.

Think about keeping your hands close, almost interlocking with each other. In this case, I wanted to carve with the tip of the blade, so my thumb is pushing on the actual blade. But you can place your thumb on the very end of the knife handle if you want to use the base of the blade when you carve.

A Whittler's Skills: The Projects

4

If there is too much crank in the spatula, it can be difficult to carve the upper side of the blade just by carving away from you. Use a long knife blade so that you can reach over the blade of the spatula, even when you are carving towards yourself.

This is a basic carving-towards-yourself grip. Hold the knife with just four of your fingers, leaving your thumb free. Hold the knife quite deep inside the palm of your hand, with the back of the blade resting in the first knuckle joint of your index finger. You can also hold the blade even deeper inside your palm, so that just the tip of the blade is protruding. But this technique is for experienced whittlers.

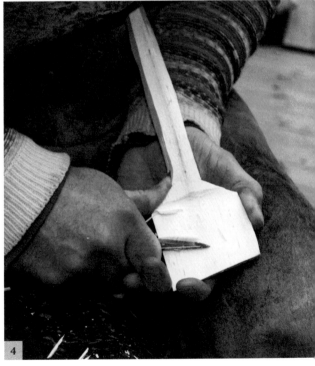

Make the cut by closing up your hand. The handle of the knife will stop when it reaches the big muscle under your thumb. The blade passes

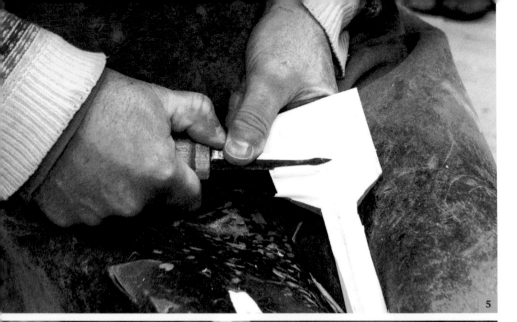

A Whittler's Skills: The Projects

above the thumb, which should be accurately positioned well below the piece of wood. This is the security rule for the grip. You can also alter the grip so that the blade never reaches your thumb in any way. It depends a little on how you angle out the knuckle joint of your thumb in relation to the big muscle under it. You will have to experiment a little with this – although not in a real situation carving with full force, of course.

5 & 6

To make longer cuts towards you; for example, when removing excess material over large distances along the handle, while still leaving a smooth and fine surface, you need another grip. A very versatile grip is to hold the piece of wood against your chest, while pulling the knife towards you, with the blade pointing up. It is obviously very easy to see what is happening as you carve, and the grip also gives great control. It is important that the blade is pointing away from you slightly, but this is something that comes naturally. It is actually really tiring on your wrist if you try to point the blade in the wrong direction. Hold the forearm of the hand holding the knife tight against your side/ribs for control and stability.

Once you have given it some practice, you can stop the grip wherever you want to – it is that controlled. The real security, however, lies in the fact that your hand/wrist will stop when it reaches your chest, with the knife pointing away from you. It is very hard to go wrong with this safety precaution in place.

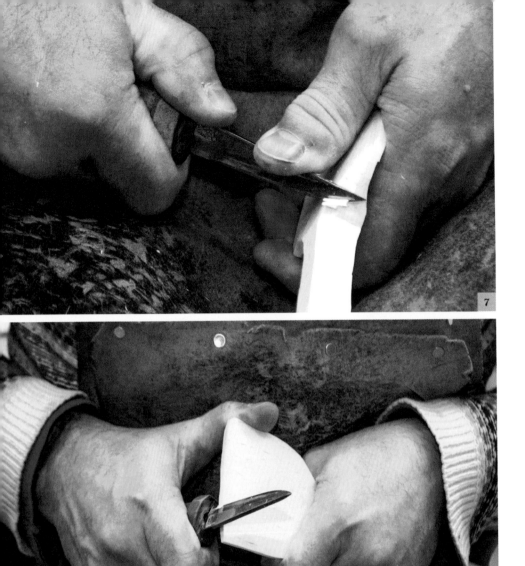

A Whittler's Skills: The Projects

7

Finish the handle and create a clean carved surface by making the cuts as controlled as you can.

8

The edge of the spatula is end-grain. Cut a little at a time or it will be too strenuous on your hand. The best technique is to carve towards your thumb, and here you can really keep your thumb out of the way.

9

A finished spatula.

9

THE BURL AND THE GUKSI: CARVING A TRADITIONAL SCANDINAVIAN DRINKING CUP

The guksi is part of the traditional Sami craft named *duodji*, which has a very distinct and outstanding system of patterns and designs that is closely related to the Sami lifestyle. The burls used to make guksis are central to the world of Sami craftwork.

Above

*Cups made from
burls by my father
and me.*

The Sami guksi

The traditional Scandinavian drinking cup or guksi, which is known as *kåsa* in Swedish, is what every outdoor person with some self-regard dreams about. Its almost magical appeal probably has something to do with its Sami context and origins. Guksi is the Sami word for a wooden drinking cup that is carried in a belt or inside a jacket and, like the knife, coffee kettle and *suophan* (the Sami "lasso"), it is considered a key part of the personal equipment of a Sami reindeer herder. It is always there whenever he or she wants a quick drink from a small stream in the high mountains or whenever there is a stop to make coffee over an open fire. It also serves as a plate, but should never be washed, just rinsed with water to get a dark matte patina on the inside.

There have been instances in the past, and perhaps to this day, when items of Sami craft have been copied and falsely sold as *duodji*. A few years ago the Duodji brand was given a grant to verify the authenticity of *duodji* made by Sami craftsmen. It is possible, however, to make a drinking cup from a burl without *ägna sig åt* – without engaging in what you might call cultural appropriation.

Although the wooden drinking cup made from a burl doesn't only exist in Sami culture, you should be careful not to incorporate the Sami patterns and reindeer antlers into your own cup designs. There is a difference between copying and taking inspiration. It was the Sami craft that first drew me into the world of woodcraft, and I often gave in to the urge to use Sami designs when making my knives or cups. But I only did so when practising my craft and for the joy of whittling.

A Whittler's Skills: The Projects

The burl

The burl is a really exclusive piece of wood. It is desired by many woodworkers, although really good burls are only found occasionally. You can admire and yearn for the beautiful burls growing on the trees in parks or someone else's garden, but it is harder to find them in the forests where you are allowed to forage. If you do happen to find a burl, you will discover that most burls have ingrowth bark elements and other defects. The perfect burl has a smooth, regular, round shape and is just the right size for a cup. If you are really lucky, the surface of the burl will also be covered with small sprouts. These sprouts result in a grain pattern called a "birds-eye pattern" – small rings and dots intermixed in the grain. This type of grain also has plenty of gleams.

What makes a burl so fantastic for making cups is that the grain follows the shape of the burl. You can make the whole cup thin without losing any strength. If you make a cup from a piece of straight wood, the edges will consist of a large amount of end-grain, and there is also a real risk of the cup cracking when you pour in hot coffee.

A burl also has cell walls that are twice as thick as those of the rest of the trunk. Of course, although this results in a cup made from a burl being extra strong, it also means that it is difficult to process. The burl must be carved when it is as fresh as possible. If the burl has been dried, it can be boiled in water to make it easier to process. I sometimes boil fresh burls as well – they can be carved like butter when hot.

Carving a cup from a burl

1

This burl dried with the bark still on it. I got this burl from a good friend and whittler who had a stroke and partially lost his mobility. So I had to finish the burl for him.

2

First check the burl for possible defects, which you will want to avoid. Remove the bark with an axe. A piece of the trunk was saved on each side of this burl to create handles, but I only wanted to keep one of them. The grain was a little spalted (colouration caused by fungi) because the bark was left on the burl while it dried; birch bark is very good at remaining moist – in fact, it is practically waterproof, which means that the wood doesn't dry very fast. This wood hadn't started to get too soft, though, and so the cup could be finished. I like to treat my wooden cups with linseed oil, as this also helps to give spalted wood additional strength.

2

3

4

5

Carve the outside of the burl with an axe to get the shape of the cup going. Remove most of the trunk from the "inside" until you reach the very pith of the burl. You will recognize this as a small ball. Create cuts with a saw to make the cutting easier. The heartwood of the burl is very hard to carve with an axe.

As this burl was dry, I boiled it in water first. To do this, let the water come to a boil with the burl in it. Then leave the burl in the hot water for a few hours. When the water has cooled, repeat the process – it takes time to soften a burl. In this case, I put the hot burl in a plastic bag overnight to keep it wet until the next day.

3

Roughly hollow out the burl with a small adze. The burl's round shape makes it difficult to fasten in a workbench for cutting, so it is best to support it with your body. Big burls/bowls can be put on the floor and held with your feet; small burls/cups can be raised slightly above the ground and held with the help of your legs, which makes burls pretty awesome to carve outside. In Sweden, taking some whittling outside is a great way of catching those short hours of winter sunlight.

You can only use the adze to carve straight down into the burl, since there is not enough room for the handle, or your arm for that matter, inside the bowl. Make the excavation from the middle and out towards the sides to get the chips out. The grain direction in a burl can never be predicted really, so the surface will be very rough in some areas. But this can be dealt with later.

If you don't have an adze, then roughly hollow out the burl with gouges, with the burl fastened in a vice or workbench. Use a wooden mallet to strike the gouge.

4

The outside of the burl is quite easy to carve with a drawknife. The best way to do this is to hold the burl against your chest while you carve. Before the inside is complete, adjust the outside and smooth out the tool marks made by the axe. When it comes to cups and bowls, it can be difficult to finish one side first and then the other – you might actually find it easier to work on both sides at the same time.

5

Don't leave the cup too thick before you dry it. It should be about the size you finally want, or you will have some very strenuous work ahead of you.

Some woodworkers choose to carve the inside with gouges. This can be very useful, especially if you use a bent gouge. Some gouges are made especially for this type of work.

Alternatively, you can use spoon knives. Big, round spoon knives are the most suitable for cups and bowls. The direction of the grain inside a burl is unpredictable, so I recommend you use a variety of spoon knives. The left-handed spoon knife can be an irreplaceable tool.

6

7

6

A carving loop with a strap allows you to work with great power, while still holding the blank in your lap/with your body. This piece of equipment is closely associated with Sami craft. And it is a tool that's customized for carving burls; you can reach into deep and narrow bowls and still work with power.

This carving technique is very special, however, and takes some getting used to. Even the best whittlers, who have been working with spoon knives for years, don't understand the ergonomics of a carving loop and strap right away. What you need to know is that all the power when you cut is going in the direction of the strap around your neck. So, the direction of the cut needs to be towards your neck. Instead of adjusting the direction of the tool, you have to adjust the piece of wood that you are working on. In other words, hold the piece of wood so you can cut in the direction of the strap, up towards your neck. The strap provides a fixed point that works as a lever for the tool. The muscles of your back and neck can pull slightly at the same time, but they are mostly just used to hold back.

7

During the drying process, there is a risk that minor cracks will appear at the edges/rim of the cup. I usually wait until the cup is dry before adjusting the rim, even if this means it is harder to carve. But the rim is not the most difficult stage of the carving. The handle can also be left until it is dry, in case it needs adjusting as a result of the drying process. However, the grain in the burl is so shifting and varied. Compression wood in the grain can make the handle bend as it dries, and so it is a good idea to have some material left for adjustments.

Drying

The drying process needs to be carried out carefully. Even if most of the material is removed, as with spoons for example, there is more tension in the grain of a burl than in a piece of straight wood. The cup should not be dried too fast. Just leaving it at room temperature will probably cause small cracks to appear in the wood.

One way to slow down the drying process is to put the cup in dry sawdust, preferably in a cool place.

The sawdust keeps the moisture from evaporating from the cup's surface too quickly and gently evens out the level of moisture. Move the cup about in the sawdust every other day so it doesn't get too confined, which can make it to go mouldy. Another method is to carefully dry the cup by putting it in a paper bag and sealing the bag tightly. The paper bag, like the sawdust, lets the moisture out gently and helps to slow down the drying process. Do not use a plastic bag to store the cup, because this will keep the wood fresh and stop it from drying (which is obviously not what you want when you are trying to dry it). Leave the cup for too long and it will start to go mouldy.

The cup can be left to dry outside to start with, in a place that doesn't get exposed to sun or wind. Keeping it outside means that the cup will dry down to outdoor humidity first and, since the air is not as dry as it is inside, the process will be gentler. I have dried wood in paper bags on the balcony and in the underground storehouse. The fridge is also an alternative if it is large enough for storing your whittlings. My favourite method is to put the cup in the insulation (sawdust) in the attic.

Keep an eye on the cup during the drying process, watching out for cracks and signs of mould.

When you have kept the cup outside for a few weeks, you will have to bring it inside to get it completely dry. Dry it at room temperature, either in sawdust or in a paper bag.

When you think the cup is dry, try holding it against your cheek: if it cools your skin, there is still moisture left in the wood; if it doesn't have a cooling effect, it is probably dry.

Once the cup is dry, it is time to finish it. Carve the outside of the cup with your knife. The grain is difficult and will chip easily. Try different spoon knives to get the inside as smooth as possible.

CARVING A SPOON

Spoon carving has become a worldwide community, with
special spoon-carving events in the UK, Australia, the US,
the Netherlands, Sweden, and elsewhere. Why spoon carving
in particular has become so popular I don't know, but it is
something that has really hit. Carving a spoon is simply a must
if you want to understand the contemporary whittling scene!
Maybe the popularity lies in the fact that the progress you
make is so obvious. Your first spoon, no matter how much
you have worked with wood before, will often look rubbish;
but then you will quickly see your spoons get better and better.

The question of whether you should make spoons from crooked
or straight wood is frequently debated. At Vindeln, where
I studied crafts, we never made spoons from straight wood.
This was always discarded as being too weak, even though
we know that throughout history people have produced huge
numbers of spoons using straight wood – and even made
a living as spoon carvers.

It wasn't until I met spoon carvers from other countries
that I came into contact with people who make beautiful
and useful spoons from straight wood. It was a relief to me
to leave behind the dogma of only using crooked wood to
make spoons. When I was teaching, I could suddenly bring
in endless quantities of material. And I could also finally
see the potential in carving spoons for selling.

When I started carving spoons for production, I sat for three
months carving six spoons a day at home in my kitchen.
I had been carving horses for a producer of the traditional
painted Dala horses, but got sick of it after a few hundred
horses. But I didn't get sick of carving spoons, and still haven't.

I had been commissioned to sell my spoons at a well-known
shop, which was stocking new designs from small brands.
I delivered 90 spoons to one of their shops in Stockholm and
had the highest of expectations. In two months they sold just
two spoons and a writer who heard about my spoons called

me "the spoon carver who carves six spoons a day and sells one a month." It was a big disappointment, but not even that stopped me from carving spoons and believing in them!

What I want to describe here is my design process. As you will see in the projects, I don't use any designs or drawings when I make my spoons. When I was carving spoons for those three months I just, at some point, started carving the same design over and over again. There was never a plan at any time to stick with it or to decide when it was ideal or finished. It was just a matter of refining the design and going on an interesting journey during that process. And, as time went by and I neglected to determine a permanent design for my spoons, I discovered that there was a benefit in that; over time, and with every spoon I carved, the design was refined and fine-tuned. This became most evident in the handle, which became more and more slender.

So, the design of your spoons can be anything you want it to be. Carving spoons can be a real challenge; the shapes are so complex and faceted. On the other hand – what if you don't make a good spoon? You just make another.

1

Spoons made from straight birch.

2

Straight maple spoons.

Cooking spoons

Cooking spoons are quite forgiving to carve; they can be thin or thick, but still useful. The surface doesn't have to be perfectly even, in contrast to an eating spoon that will go in your mouth, where you will feel the slightest splinter or chipping in the surface. A cooking spoon is also a good carving size for the axe work.

Making the blank

Even though making the blank may seem to be quite a small part of the process, it is actually a big part of the work involved in making a spoon.

I am part of a group of people in Järvsö that comes together twice a month to sit and carve – it is totally disorganized, just random carving. Anyway, a very interested young man named Simon started joining us. He was carving a spoon from a big pine branch. I watched as he struggled with the monstrous lump, but I didn't want to take the teaching role and so said nothing. Then he went on a short course that we run and, after I had shown him how to axe out a blank, he came back with one beautiful, elegant spoon after another.

He also learned how to create a razor-sharp edge on one of his carving axes and, as he was shaving off a few hairs from his arm with it, he exclaimed, "This is a real dad-thing!" He went on to say, "When someone has a bad axe, people will tell them to 'take it to Simon, he can fix it.'"

1

To make the blank, you first need to split a piece of wood. This is similar to the work involved when making a spatula (see page 74). You can make the blank for the spoon from a half, a quarter, or an even smaller section, depending on how big the tree was.

Use either of the two-eighths. For this project, I worked on the triangular section and hollowed the spoon from the side where the bark was.

The width of the blank determines how wide the spoon will be, but the sides can be carved down a little. It is also a good idea to make the blank a little more square, rather than triangular – this will make it easier to control the shape of the spoon.

2

This is the back of the blank. Make two different cuts to shape the slight crank in the blade of the spoon: the first one should be a kind of crosscut

A Whittler's Skills: The Projects

made where the blade and handle meet, while the second should be made from the edge of the blade and towards the crosscut.

3

Use the axe to make a crosscut where you want the blade to start. To make the axe cut into the wood, position it at a slight angle, but don't worry too much about being precise with this.

4

Hold the blank horizontally on the block and make a cut sideways across the fibres. This method of cutting is similar to the way in which you hew timber. It is a very effective way of cutting a flat surface, because the wood is easier to cut across the fibres. However, without the first crosscut, the wood would just break off all the way up to the handle. Make sure you get a slight crank in the blade and that the axe head is not loose. This cut is not

made with a great deal of power; you need full control. Keep your arms close to your body and just move your forearm up and down, using your elbow as a fixed point.

5

Size down the handle a little before making a crosscut at the point where the blade and handle meet.

6

Carefully carve down towards the crosscut. Try to stop half an inch before the crosscut and break off the last fibre. Repeat the process for the other side of the handle.

7

Take away some more material from the back of the blade and from the handle. Make sure you take away from those areas that will give most crank to the spoon. Keep the meeting point of the blade and handle low and the tips (of the handle and blade) high.

5

6

7

A Whittler's Skills: The Projects

Using the adze

1

A spoon knife is not a very efficient tool, to be honest, and the worst aspect of using it is making the first excavation into the roughed-out blade. So, some spoon carvers prefer to use an adze for the initial hollowing of the blade. The adze should not be too heavy and have a short handle. The hollowing is made from the sides and towards the middle.

Make the first cut from the back of the blade, almost straight down. Make your cuts swift, but not that powerful. Too much force will actually break the blade. In this case, once the blank was nearly finished, there wasn't much material left to remove.

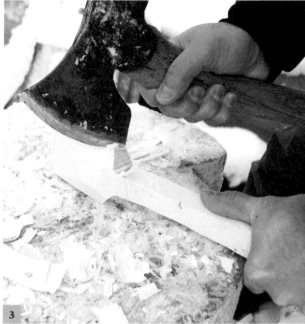

2

Make the cuts meet in the middle to undo the chips.

Use the adze to make a start for the spoon knife, but not to finish the hollowing in any way – it is too heavy and cannot create the tight curves needed for this. However, starting off the hollowing with an adze is a good idea if the blanks are going to be dried, and just taking away a little with the adze will be enough in this instance.

3

Smooth the sharp corners left from the crosscuts on the back of the blade with the lower tip of the axe, to help make carving easier later.

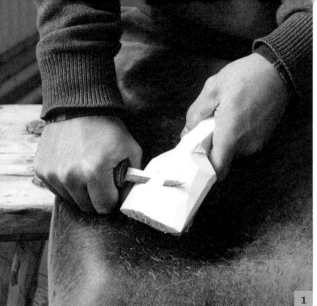

1

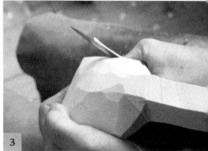

2

3

Clean carving

Once the blank has been roughed out, it can either be dried or finished while still raw. From now on, the work is done with a knife and spoon knives.

1

First carve the back of the blade, removing the traces from the axe and straightening up the shape. The most efficient grip for this is to carve away from you, using the strength of your shoulder to press the blade down.

2

It is best to carve the very tip of the spoon by pushing with your thumb. I prefer this method because it makes the blade of the spoon a little convex (a convex shape can be difficult to achieve with a knife grip that's too powerful).

3

Carve the outside curve of the blade. The transition between the

A Whittler's Skills: The Projects

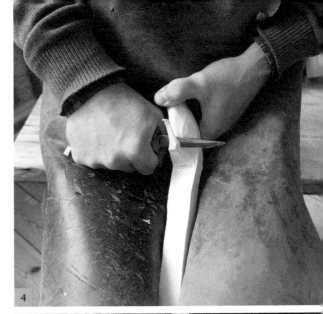

blade and the handle is a vital part of the spoon, so you should have control of that before starting on the inside of the blade. Carving towards your body, with the spoon supported by your chest, is a good, powerful, but controlled grip.

4

This is a controlled way of carving away from you; your knife hand is pressing down onto your leg, leaving only limited room for movement. "Roll" the knife forwards and push it slightly through the wood at the same time. As the cut finishes, the handle of the knife will be touching the spoon blank.

5

This grip gives you great control over the movement of the blade.

6

The transition from the blade to the handle is often too undefined. Make sure you keep it nice and tight.

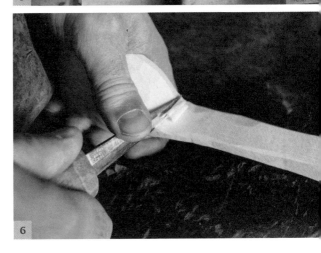

Carving a Spoon

Using the spoon knife

When you have finished the back of the blade, and cleared the transition between the blade and the handle of traces from the axe, it is time to carve the inside of the blade. In other words, it is time to bring out the spoon or hook knife, whichever term you prefer. Of course, you can do this whenever you want, but I like to carve a spoon in this working order. It is easier to adjust the handle than the blade, so I like to save the handle until last and have some extra material there that I can adjust.

The inside of the spoon can be carved with just one spoon knife, but it is usual to have a right- and left-handed one, as they complement each other: where one of them has a problem reaching, the other might be useful.

The diversity of grips is not as wide as for a knife, but a spoon knife definitely needs some getting used to. The first time I used one, I put it very cleanly in my thumb. So start gently.

Most spoon knives come with a short handle. I prefer to buy mine without a handle so that I can make the handle myself – I like to make it a little longer. This gives you a wider range of grips to choose from.

The spoon knife is preferably used lightly, and should not grab too much. A mistake many beginners make is to go in too sharp with the edge and then they just get stuck. It is better to go in with a shallow angle, really resting on the full bevel, and to take small cuts, especially to start with, before you get a cavity going. A successful way to use the spoon knife is to really

A Whittler's Skills: The Projects

twist the knife when you carve, so that the chips don't get stuck and you end up tearing the surface rather than carving it.

1

This is the basic carving grip to use for a spoon knife: hold the knife with the blade pointing towards you, grab the handle with just four fingers, and then pull the knife towards your thumb, but aim over it. The cut is finished when the handle of the knife stops inside your palm. Keep your thumb low, just in case.

2

Use a "left-handed" spoon knife by holding it in your right hand (that is, if you are right-handed; if you are left-handed, the reverse applies), with the edge pointing away from you. Use the thumb of the other hand to push on the blade. The left-handed spoon knife is really good for reaching the back of the spoon.

I often use it to carve the sharp curve in the back of the blade and down to the bottom. The hand holding the knife can concentrate on twisting the tool in a swift motion, as the other hand pushes the tool.

3

This is a very useful grip and one that's usually mastered after you have gained some experience. It is easier to perform if you have a longer handle on the blade. Hold the knife in your right hand – again, if you are right-handed – with the blade pointing towards you. During the cut you really have two forces pushing the blade through the wood: the fingers of your left hand on the blade or the very end of the knife handle and your right hand pushing on the handle like a lever around your left hand.

4

The finished spoon.

The spoons that went missing for 13 years...

In 2004, I sent some spoons to an old friend who wanted to sell craftwork in the studio that she had just started. Thirteen years later, when I began working on this book, I got a text message saying that she wanted to send the spoons back to me. I had no memory of them and thought they would just be useless, mediocre practice examples to me now. So I replied that it wasn't necessary. "But I have already bought a box," she texted back.

And then a box arrived containing two birch-bark boxes, three letter openers inspired by the great artist/whittler Jemt-Olov, from Orsa, and two really big ladles carved from birch crooks. The ladles were totally representative of the types of spoons I made at the time. I didn't believe in making eating spoons, since I didn't use them myself. But I couldn't resist a really big birch crook when I saw one. I recall one beautiful spring day when I was out with a friend hiking in the woods, collecting birch for an activity of some kind. We took a break in the warm moss and lay in the sun while he told stories from his long life. On the way back, with big loads of birch in our arms, we passed one of the most perfect, really big birch crooks I had ever seen. I said, "Oh no, I won't be able to carry it!" But my friend said, "You have to take it!" So, one of those ladles in the box could have been that crook!

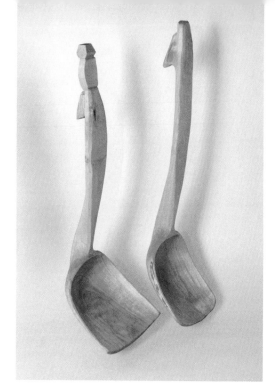

What surprised me when I opened the box was that I was clearly a much more skilled spoon carver than I recall having been.

My favourite types of crooks are the ones with a really tight curve – I used to describe them as being shaped like a gutter. They make nice servers.

The crook is first split through the pith and the inner half is used to make the spoon. It is carved so that the bottom of the blade follows the curve of the wood. With an intact fibre following the spoon, the very thinnest part of the spoon – the blade (and especially the tip) – is kept very strong, even though it has a really aggressive crank in it.

A SMALL SHELF:
SOME SIMPLE JOINERY

Small, beautiful, richly decorated shelves were found in most old farmhouses in Sweden. The small shelf would hold all the farm's books and valuable documents. The books usually included the Bible and a hymn book. These shelves are, in fact, sometimes called hymn-book shelves. They would have several shelves and a drawer. A characteristic of hymn-book shelves is their open gables; instead of solid sides made from boards, the shelves are held together or supported by a pole at each corner. As well as the poles holding the construction together, there might also be poles purely for decoration. This is why it's so rewarding to make a hymn-book shelf for yourself. It is an architectural challenge and the decorative elements are integral to the function of the object and not just there as added details.

The shelf sequence shown on the following pages is simple enough, with four poles and two shelves, and demonstrates just one of the ways in which shelves can be joined. The joinery is made from a cross-halving joint with housed corners. It might sound complicated but is, in fact, quite basic. I have seen this type of joint in shelves that are regarded as folk art. It doesn't only belong in guild carpentry and is made with a few simple tools. The housed corners give the shelf stability; if the joints are not stable, the shelf will start to sag when hung on the wall and weighed down with books, and so on. So, the joints need to be quite tight. However, since there are eight joints in the shelf, they help to stabilize each other. The tension between the different parts will also even out any joints that are a little weak.

The two pieces for the shelves can be split from fresh wood and then dried and flattened with an axe and hand plane. They can also be made from reclaimed wood.

Above

A shelf by Niklas Karlsson, decorated with linseed-oil paint.

Making the shelf

1

I made the two shelves from a board of reclaimed wood. They measured 450 x 180mm (18 x 7in). Use a set square to cut the edges at 90-degree angles, after you have planed one side straight. Flatten one side of each board, using two different types of planes: one long trying plane to flatten the peaks and then a smaller smoothing plane that won't remove much wood, but will give a really smooth surface.

2

Once one side is flat, mark the thickness of each shelf using the flat side as a guide. I made a facet on each side, down to the line, which left a high ground in the middle. This made it easier to remove the material quickly. This technique is similar to when you are cutting with an axe and want to remove large, flat surfaces.

3

Once the shelves are flattened and the edges and measures adjusted (so you have two equally sized shelves), you need to make the notches to support the poles. The notches should be 10mm (⅜in) wide and 20mm (¾in) deep. Do not place them too close to the edges. I positioned them 20mm (¾in) in. Measure and draw the notches. Use a set square, if necessary. Make two saw cuts and then remove the

wood with a chisel. Be careful not to remove all the wood at once. Make small cuts. Use a wooden mallet to strike the chisel. Protect your workbench with a piece of board. To prevent chips from breaking off, cut the notch from both sides.

4

Once the shelves are finished, prepare the four pieces of wood for the poles. The pieces should measure 340 x 30 x 22mm (13 x 1 x ⅞in). I marked the centre of each pole and then marked up 24cm (9½in). This is the space between the shelves – in other words, the notches in the poles will be 24cm (9½in) apart. Since the shelves are planed by hand, they can vary a little in thickness, which means the notches should be fitted individually. Decide which pole will go into which notch and mark the poles so that you can keep track of them.

Take the first pole and mark up the respective width of the notch and the thickness of the shelf. Make two saw cuts from the sides of the pole and use a knife to remove the wood. Make sure the notches are not too wide; it is better to adjust them with a knife to get a really tight fit. Try to press the pole into the notch in the shelf, using a wooden mallet to gently strike it down. Repeat this process for the remaining three poles.

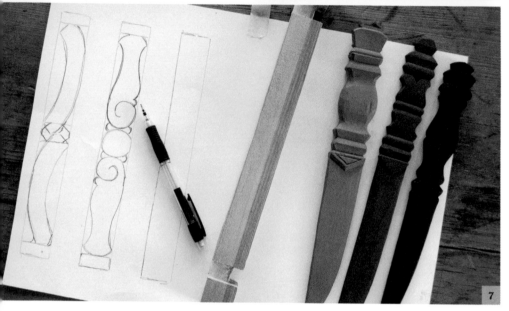

5 & 6

Adjust the notches with the knife to ensure that each pole fits. Repeat until each pole fits tightly, but be careful, because too much force will break something. Finish one joint at a time until they are all done and tested before you assemble the shelf.

Making the joints for the construction of the shelves might be tedious, but the reward is the whittling of the poles and seeing the shelves come to life afterwards. It is a moment of sparkling anticipation when all four poles are ready and waiting to be put in place.

7

To carve the poles for this hymn-book shelf, or for making furniture and joinery, for example, I recommend you make a plan first. This isn't necessary when carving spoons or whittling other small items, because the key to creating freely as you go along is training your sense of form and the interplay between your eyes and hands. However, it is a little too much of a gamble to start randomly carving larger items when so much work has been done. Still, you don't need to complicate things too much. Just take one of the poles and outline the shape on a piece of paper, and then sketch out a few design ideas.

A Whittler's Skills: The Projects

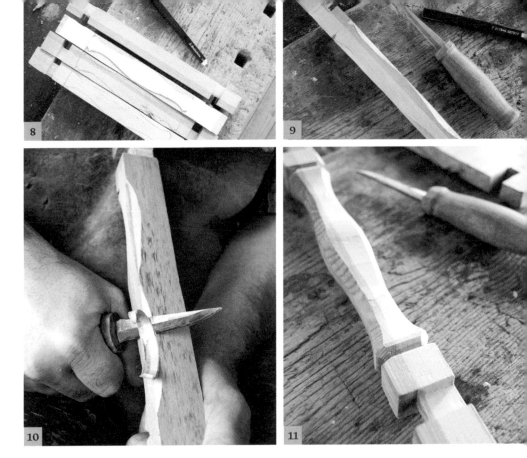

I suggest finding something to inspire you – perhaps look at some antiques, go to a museum or simply look in a book or magazine.

8

Once you have decided on a shape for the poles, make a primitive template; it doesn't have to be that detailed and can be drawn directly onto the wood.

9

When carving three-dimensional shapes, rough out the shape first. Remove wood where the shape tapers or hollows. Also, start by marking the ends of the different segments in the shape. Make crosscuts with a knife to cut the fibres where you want the next cut to stop. This will stop chips from breaking off.

10

Carve from two directions and meet at the lowest point to create the curves in the design.

11

Try to carve distinct lines. The facets from the knife will give life to the surface of the wood.

12

If you've decorated and carved the poles, the shelves can look a little bland if they aren't given some kind of shaping, too. You can use a moulding plane to add lines and give life to the shelves. These planes can be found in antique shops or secondhand markets. The tool fetishist will enjoy using a moulding plane; they can be a challenge to get to work well. The most important thing is that the blade should follow the shape of the base of the plane.

13

Add a thin moulding to the sides of the shelves to make them look more complete. This is how chest lids are constructed. The mouldings for this small shelf can be nailed into place with wooden pegs, whereas the mouldings for chests need to be joined.

14

The finished hymn-book shelf.

A Whittler's Skills: The Projects

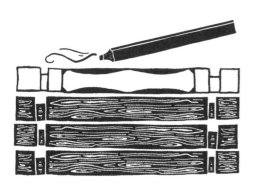

1

This is the
moulding plane
steel and base
seen directly
from the front.

2

This shows the
front edge of one
of the shelves.

3

A moulding plane.

A WHITTLED PEG RACK

A peg rack is useful in any house. In old farmhouses, they are a mandatory part of the hall's interior. They can stretch along a whole wall and be used to keep lots of handy things organized and accessible. As a whittling project, making a peg rack is full of possibilities in terms of design and ornamentation. The backboard can be minimalist straight or curvaceous, decorated with chip carving or mouldings, or perhaps painted, and so on. The same choices apply to the pegs.

I found some old peg racks in the sheds at my old house. The simplest design had completely straight round pegs. They were drilled into the board at a slight angle, pointing up, so that whatever was hung on them wouldn't slip off. Another one was made with quite long, round, straight pegs, with a small hook at the end.

A quite common shape for pegs, however – and I think this design is really nice – is a short rectangular peg that tapers in a steep slope before ending in a distinct knob. There was a long peg rack with this type of peg in my woodshed. I will use that design for this project. The peg rack shown here is made from recycled wood, namely a piece of barn board from an old shed that was torn down. The rack is quite short, so can be carved with just a knife.

1

A new peg rack in the style of an old model.

2

An old peg rack.

3

New peg racks with simple straight pegs. The holes are drilled at an angle to prevent coats from falling off.

Making the peg rack

1

My piece of barn board was really weathered and didn't look like much but, on closer inspection, I discovered that the wear was just shallow and that underneath not more than a fraction of a millimetre of the wood was fresh, while the old pine had turned a beautiful red.

Split the board so that you have a piece of wood about 5cm (2in) wide. You can split the wood with an axe or even a knife. Take a knife and a wooden mallet or hammer (if you don't mind hitting your knife with it) and split the board as for the spatula and spoon blanks (see pages 75 and 98, respectively). If the board doesn't split when you have struck down the whole blade of the knife, prise the wood apart by twisting the knife hard.

2

Carve the sides straight and parallel by supporting the piece of wood against the chopping block while pushing down with the knife. Make sure that only the blade of the knife stops at the chopping block – it will hurt to punch your knuckles into the block repeatedly.

3

Carve the backboard for the peg rack with the knife. A plane might seem the most appropriate tool, but this depends on the conditions and what equipment you have. The knife grip shown here is the most efficient and the one that I prefer.

4

Mark the position of the pegs on the backboard. Save an inch or so at the sides to stop the wood cracking when you drill the holes and fit the pegs. The distance between the pegs should be about 10cm (4in). Distribute the number of pegs you want evenly between the two outer pegs.

5

Drill the holes in the backboard. I used an old drill with a spoon bit to drill the holes. Since the surface of the backboard was carved with a knife, you might find that it is not completely level and even. So, use your eye as a measure when you drill. If you put a set square on the board, it might not sit straight.

Put a piece of wood underneath the board so that you don't drill down into the workbench.

When holding the drill in position, aim down the drill to ensure you are not pushing it forwards or backwards, and that the drill is not leaning to either side. Try to hold the drill as straight as possible. Lock your body in position as you drill. Since the pegs are not that long, a small inclination might not be detectable with the naked eye. Drill the holes all the way through the board.

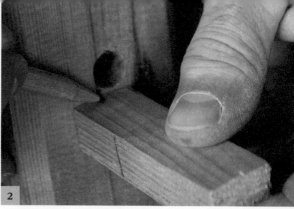

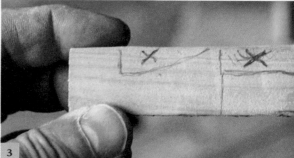

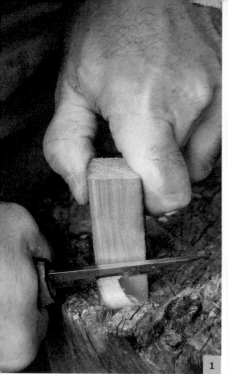

Making the peg tenons

1

To make the blanks for the pegs, I used a saw to cut off short pieces from the remaining piece of barn board. Each peg has a tenon that goes into the board, so the full length of the blank needs to include the tenon (that is, the thickness of the board). Carve the pegs into a rectangular shape first, using the chopping block to support the peg as you carve straight down.

2

Mark the thickness of the board and the diameter of the hole on the peg. You now have the size for the tenon.

3

The marked-up peg.

4

Start by carving the tenon. Press the knife down into the sharp corner of the peg, where the tenon starts.

5

Make another cut down towards the first, to start forming the shoulder above the tenon.

6

Carve down the rest of the sharp corner, diagonally from the centre of the top and down to the line. When the cut is finished, repeat the cuts on the opposite side.

7

You now have a high edge along the top. Take away the material in the same way as before, down to the line, until you have a square tenon.

A Whittler's Skills: The Projects

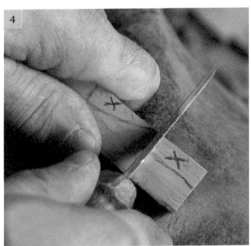

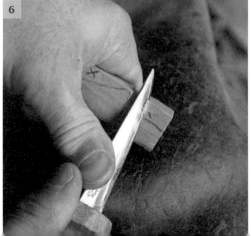

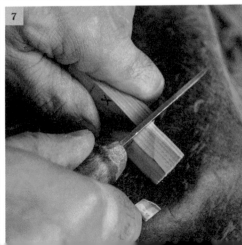

8 9

10 11 12

8

The tenon should now be the same size as (or slightly wider than) the diameter of the hole, only square in shape.

9

Carve the tip of the tenon to make it round. Don't work on more than a few millimetres at the front of the tenon. Carefully remove the material until you can press the top of the tenon into the hole. Press and turn the peg – this will compress the wood at the end of the tenon, leaving a mark from the hole.

10

From the compressed wood at the top of the tenon, you can see exactly what shape the tenon will have. Pare down the material with the knife. Test the tenon repeatedly by pressing it into the hole during this process. When the tenon is completed and fits into the hole, carve the rest of the peg.

11

The pegs are quite small and hard to hold while carving. Carving against the thumb and pushing with the thumb on the blade are the two most suitable grips for this.

12

Carve the rough shape first. Carve facets and make crosscuts.

A Whittler's Skills: The Projects

13

13

The finished peg rack with all the pegs carved and attached. The pegs can be wedged from the back so that they fit really tightly. Take a knife and press to make a small notch in the peg. Make a small wedge, very thin and sharp, which is the same width as the peg. Make the notch straight across the grain of the board, or the wedge will have a splitting effect. Make sure the peg is held firmly against the surface or it will loosen from the board when you strike the wedge. Hit the wedge with a hammer until it feels as if it is tight. Be resolute with the hammer, but not reckless.

14

14

Notice the position of the wedge in relation to the grain of the board.

FÅGELSJÖ AND THE BIRCH-BARK BOX

Fågelsjö – also called *Bortom Åa* (meaning "beyond the river") – in Hälsingland, Sweden, is one of UNESCO's World Heritage Site farms. It was built when the Finns colonized the area in the 1600s. The last owner bequeathed the farm to the municipality and it is now a centre for craft in the region, as well as a hostel, tourist attraction, museum and general point of interest.

I first went to Fågelsjö in the late 1990s, as an assistant on a whittling course held by renowned carver Janne Eliasson. The nature and surroundings were magical to me, as well as the deep and ever-present craft tradition of the place. The settlers inhabiting the farm have taken advantage of the natural resources in a way that is truly inspiring. The land is full of red soil, and they have welded rifle barrels from bog iron ore in the smithy. There is a shed with seven locks, and the villagers still make sour dace (a fish rarely eaten nowadays), which is fermented in the underground storehouses.

This is a place where stories live on and where time flows in a different way. I once enrolled on a course on making birch-bark boxes at Bortom Åa. At the time, I was living in Järvsö, 60 miles (95km) from Fågelsjö, and the course was supposed to start on a Friday evening. I had planned to leave work early, but had to stay, so I rushed home, packed the car and drove as fast as I could over the mountains and vast forests. When I pulled up at Bortom Åa, with a bad excuse ready, the hostel manager and course leader, Brita, greeted me with a big smile. "Some of the members of your course decided to play boules tonight. So we decided to start tomorrow morning instead," she told me. And I felt such relief to be in a place where there was no concept of stress.

A Whittler's Skills: The Projects

1

*The porch at
Fågelsjö.*

2

*Boxes made
by Nils Blixt.*

One of the most amazing things about this place is that when the last owners of the old farmhouse at Bortom Åa built a new house, they ensured that everything in the old house was preserved. This was in the early 1900s, when open-air museums and folk museums, such as Skansen in Stockholm, were built due to a growing interest in ethnology. And you can see a big difference between the folklore museums that were installed and furnished with collected items to look authentic and Bortom Åa. In the old farmhouse in Fågelsjö, there are 13 rifles hanging on the kitchen wall – all made on the farm. On a shelf above the door, there are 18 turned bowls; on the same wall, there are 11 big ladles hanging from a rack. The shed with seven locks is filled with coopered vessels and, where the farmhand lived in another house that had stables and a coach house, there are countless numbers of scythes, fishing nets and other pieces of equipment. The stories of the farm's inhabitants come to life in all these items; they are things produced by generations who needed to make their own tools in order to survive.

On all the courses I attended, there was always one essential thing, one rule that had to be followed: never rush, never be hasty, enjoy the moment. One summer it rained for two weeks. I was holding courses for families where the children and the parents did things together, and it rained every evening, but on a few nights it stopped raining late at night. And we thought: "Now it stops." But the next morning, it would be pouring down again. Out in the field it looked as though the cows were strolling in the high grass, but it was actually 15cm (6in) of water. All the roads had been damaged by rain. But the children on the course gladly joined in the expeditions and explorations around the forests of Fågelsjö. As we were exploring a great canyon in the woods, we started to look for troll settlements in the moss and rocks that we passed.

MAKING A
BIRCH-BARK BOX

Opposite

*Taking birch bark
in Fågelsjö.*

The Finns that settled in Sweden in the 1600s brought a great knowledge of birch bark with them. For me, Fågelsjö and birch bark are closely linked. When I think of Fågelsjö, I think of birch bark: the wonderful boxes in the old farmhouse; the seminar about sewn bark containers held by Ingalill Eliasson; the courses I held myself the week before midsummer, when the birch bark can be harvested. And meeting Nils Blixt, who was one of Sweden's most renowned birch-bark artists. Nils Blixt died some years ago, but left a great treasure trove of fantastic work. He was most known for his birch-bark boxes.

Nils Blixt made exquisite birch-bark boxes. He was a little dogmatic about them, and had a set of rules by which he lived. Most importantly for him, a birch-bark box should not be glued. And because it is not glued, it has to be sewn with birch root at the top to hold the two sheets together. He also had firm opinions on the lid and how the joint should be made. He said that the joint should be cut with a knife, preferably freehand in order to adapt to the material. He wanted nothing aggressive in his boxes, no sharp edges, no straight cuts.

Nils Blixt's boxes were requested by many people, largely because he held on to them so dearly. He rarely sold any boxes at the start of his whittling career, which began when he took early retirement from his job as a painter. He often told people how his life became easy and enjoyable once he started with the craft. He said it was downhill from then on. It was easy to live. He also told people that it wasn't really him that made his boxes; it was "the determiner". His boxes were richly decorated with stories that he picked up from the birch bark itself, the different patterns he could see and brought out in the wood. As his production grew larger, he started selling more boxes, although some remained in his home. And some are in Fågelsjö.

Gathering the box material

Birch bark is harvested for a few weeks in the summer, around midsummer time. The sap rises early in the spring, but the birch bark doesn't come loose until later. The bark is harvested by making an incision down the trunk of the tree. The cut doesn't have to be more than a few millimetres deep. After this, I usually try to press the back of my knife under the bark and gently loosen the first centimetre or so along the incision. When I can get my fingers in to grab the bark, I pull it loose from the cambium (the inner bark). The sheets have to be stored flat and pressed down with weights; otherwise they will curl in on themselves and it's impossible to get them flat again.

Making the box

You need two sheets of birch bark to make one box: one on the outside and one on the inside. The outside, with the joint, is prepared first. When you work with birch bark, it is a good idea to wet it with water – not soak it, but simply wet it with your hands now and then.

1

I like to use as much of the sheet as possible, which means that the size of your box will depend on the size of the sheet of birch bark. The box shouldn't be too high, though, compared to the width. You want to keep a sense of proportion. In this case, the sheet for the box was 21cm (8¼in) high and had a total length of 55cm (21½in). Make sure that the sheet is rectangular in shape. Scrape the surface with a worn-out knife. (Some people like to use a wood rasp, while others just use their fingers to peel off the layers.)

2

Use a knife with a curved tip to make the edges of the sheet a little thinner. The curve will help you to make precise cuts.

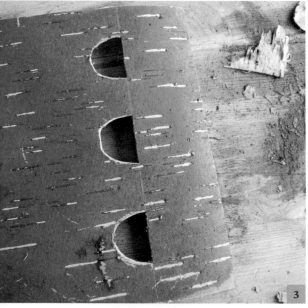

3

Take a set square and draw a line on the sap side of the sheet, about 5cm (2in) in from each short side. Mark three semi-circular notches on the line. According to Nils Blixt, this stage should be done without measuring and making sure everything is symmetrical. What you need to consider, however, are the eyes of the birch bark. The eyes are the small, darker lines that run horizontally across the sheet. These are the bark's weak spots and tend to crack and break if handled too recklessly. (So, the fewer and the shorter the eyes are on a piece of birch bark, the better its quality.) Make sure you don't have an eye in the corner of the notches, for example. Try to place the notches between the eyes as much as possible. Cut the notches with a knife. If the birch bark is very tough, you might have to score repeatedly. Ensure the knife doesn't slip away by locking your arms towards your body and making controlled cuts. It can be a good idea to push the knife with your thumb. Study this photograph carefully – the semi-circles should be placed on the correct side of the line.

4

Roll the sheet into a cylinder, with both lines matching up. The side with the notches should be rolled on top of the side without any notches. Use a couple of clothes pegs to hold the sheet in position. Use an awl to make a hole in the lower piece of birch bark in each corner of the notches. Now you have transferred the exact measurements of the notches to the other side of the sheet.

A Whittler's Skills: The Projects

5

Cut out the notches on the other side of the sheet using the punched holes as your guide – this is something of an intelligence test because it is hard to "see" the shape when you are doing it. For this reason, it is very easy to turn the notches the wrong way and remove the wrong material. Cut the notches diagonally from each other and on the "inside" of the line.

6

Once you have cut out the notches on both sides, cut them open on one side to form the tongues in the joint. I usually make the tongues on the side with two half-notches. Cut a few millimetres in from the corner, since it is very important to leave a little shoulder, to act as a hook. Make the tongues slightly tapered.

7

Fold the sheet until the notches and tongues meet. The tongues will be pushed into the notches and hooked on the inside, but they can't be pushed in all at once. Bend the tongues slightly, as you push them into the notches. When you bend birch bark in this way, it can break easily, so be gentle and take it slowly, a little at a time, until the three tongues are completely pushed through.

8

This is what the inside of the box looks like when the tongues are pushed through and locked in position.

9

Clean another sheet of birch bark and thin out the edges. It must be long enough for the ends to overlap

a little when rolled into a cylinder and placed inside the first sheet. Make this sheet a few millimetres taller than the outside sheet, to give a little material for making adjustments. Roll up the sheet, with the sap-side facing inwards, put it inside the outer cylinder, and let it expand. Squeeze the two cylinders together tightly. The overlaps should be placed on opposite sides.

10

Once you have finished making the cylinder for the box, put it under a press to dry and keep its shape. Make a last from two half-logs (the easiest way to do this is, of course, to split a log and use the two halves). The last should fit easily inside the tube. This means you don't have to make them exact. Make two large wedges and then push the log halves apart by using a mallet or hammer to drive the wedges in between them at both ends of the tube. Let the cylinder sit in the last overnight or for longer.

11

Carefully remove the cylinder from the last. Remember that the inner sheet is still just loose inside the outer sheet. They usually stick together when dried under a press, but will come loose again quite easily.

Place the cylinder on a piece of wood, about 15mm (⅝in) thick. Draw inside the cylinder with a pen and cut out the base for the box with a saw. Carve the edges until the base can be pressed inside the cylinder with a tight fit. Taper the edge of the base to make the fitting easier and prevent damage to the cylinder.

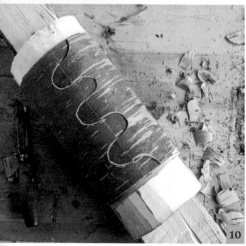

A Whittler's Skills: The Projects

12

Let the bottom of the cylinder extend a few millimetres below the base. The box will then rest on the soft birch-bark cylinder instead of the wooden base, and so will feel much softer and quieter when it is set down on a table. This is one of Nils Blixt's rules for making birch-bark boxes.

13

Split some small wooden nails from a piece of densely grown wood (in this case, I used old pine).

14

Using a 3-mm (⅛-in) drill bit, drill holes through the birch bark and into the base of the box. Carve the nails so that they will fit in the holes. Make the nails the same size as the diameter of the holes in the box (that is, 3mm/⅛in), but square. A square nail in a round hole makes for a really strong joint.

15

The two sheets can be sewn together at the top with birch root. The birch root reinforces the bark, which would otherwise start to split and peel. It is also very decorative. You can dig up birch root where the birch trees are growing in soft soil. The long, straight roots are stripped of bark, rolled up and saved. When you come to use the birch root, soak it in water for a few minutes first.

11

12

13

14

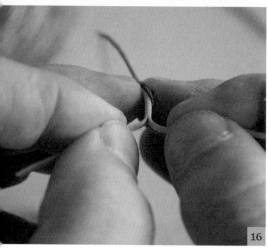

16

Split the root into two halves. Split the first 1cm (½in) or so with a knife. Then grab each end with your index fingers and thumbs. I like to use my middle fingers to hold the root in a steady grip. This really helps. Pull the ends apart in a slow and controlled manner. If one end is getting thinner, try to pull more on the other (thicker) end. This is the same principle as when you are splitting wood. If one side is pushed away more, it will get thinner. So, you can control the splitting by pulling more on either of the sides. You might have to practise this technique a little. But don't worry – it is very easy to splice the root.

17

Begin sewing by making a hole in the layers of birch bark with an awl 5mm (³/₁₆in) from the top. Push the awl from the outside in. Point the end of the root a little and then push it through the hole. If you just get the pointed tip through, grab it and pull. Leave 20mm (¾in) of the root poking out. Fold the remaining end over the top of the cylinder and tuck it in between both layers. Make the next hole 5mm (³/₁₆in) from the first, but not level with it. Position it

A Whittler's Skills: The Projects

17

closer to or further down from the top. Fold the root over the rim and push it through the next hole. Pull tight. Continue to sew from the outside, pulling the root tight as you go over the rim and back into the next hole.

Wet the root continuously as you sew. If it gets too dry, it will break. To splice the root, cut it off and start with a new root in the previous hole so that they overlap. Once the root is dry, it won't move or unravel. Do the same when you finish the sewing.

18

18

This is the finished top of the box, clearly showing the sewing technique.

19

Make the lid of the box in the same way as the base, although Nils Blixt preferred to make a ledge. Birch bark is a little elastic, and so over time a lid without a ledge to act as a stop will need to be pressed further and further down, as the birch bark stretches out.

19

Put the box, with the top side facing down, on a piece of wood and trace around it with a pen. It's nice if the lid is a little cupped, so make the lid thicker than the base. Cut out the lid with a saw. Estimate how thick the wall of the box is, with the root-stitching included, and draw the inner diameter of the lid. Mark a line around the side of the lid, which determines how far the lid can be pushed down into the box: in other words, how deep the ledge is (around 1cm/²/₅in is recommended).

A Whittler's Skills: The Projects

20

Fasten the lid in a workbench or a
vice with the lid standing on end.
With a fine saw, make a saw-cut
around the lid down to the line
marking the inner diameter of the
box. With a thin chisel, or with the
edge of a larger chisel, remove the
wood below the saw-cut. Don't
cut all the way at once. The final
adjustment of the lid can be made
with a knife. It is important that
the lid is tight. The root-stitching
around the top of the box will
mould to the lid when the lid is
pressed into place.

20

Here are two of my finished
birch-bark boxes.

DECORATIVE WOODCARVING

A knife and a piece of wood give you a sense of freedom to do whatever you want, and many people find the urge to decorate irresistible. The most common way to decorate a piece of wood is to start "drawing" with the tip of the knife. Slightly more elaborate patterns are possible with chip carving. This is a crash course in both techniques, but the basics are really not that complicated.

Above

A smaller knife is useful when decorating. Only the tip of the blade is used.

From top to bottom: A ground-down Mora slöjd knife, which has a pointy blade that is useful for making thin lines; a chip-carving knife, which has a straight blade with a fairly blunt tip; a small ornament knife that is really good for carving fine lines.

Carving decorative lines

1

Using a pencil, draw the decorative lines you want to cut first. Try to draw the lines in one stroke and create a thin, neat line each time.

2

Carve on one side of the line, but imagine that the tip of the blade is right underneath the line. In other words, hold the knife at a slight angle. Push the blade into the wood by a few millimetres. Here, I'm holding the knife like a pen. Your hand should rest steadily on the surface. Try to carve in as controlled a manner as you can. The knife must not slip away!

3

Instead of using a pen grip, you can also use an adapted carving-towards-your-thumb grip. Use the thumb of your knife hand to provide support and control.

4

5

4

When you have made a cut on one side of the line, make a cut from the other side. Keep outside the line, but imagine the tip going straight underneath the line. This cut should meet the first cut in the middle and a small strip of wood should come loose. I started with the easy parts to remove the pencil line as efficiently as I could. I didn't want to smudge the wood.

5

This is the V-shaped groove carved with the knife. You can use a V-shaped gouge instead, but this tends to tear the fibres and won't leave the same sharp cuts.

6

A breadboard with carved decorative lines.

Chip carving

1

Chip carving is often associated with carving triangular-shaped chips. The technique only involves three cuts. Use a pen to make a small dot in order to mark the tip of the triangle. In this way, you can mark out a pattern without the risk of smudging the wood.

Position the tip of the blade at the tip of the triangle (the dot). Press the tip of the blade down, at an angle of around 45 degrees, leaving a cut that is about as long as it is deep and declining.

2

Make another cut in the same way, so that it meets the first cut at the dot, but turn the knife by 90 degrees.

3

This photograph shows cuts one and two.

4

Finish the shape by making a third cut from one corner of the triangle down to the tip. Push the tip of the knife down one side and make sure that the line between the two corners is straight and neat.

5

Chip carving on the handle of a breadboard.

6

A breadboard made from birch, then carved with decorations and finished with linseed oil.

FINISHING

For some time, finishing was my main worry. I wanted
to achieve something specific, but I didn't know how; the
smooth, deep matte colours on the antiques, the feeling of old
wallpaintings, or the churches' interior decorations. When
you choose finishing techniques for your whittled objects, you
want something that ages with beauty. I have concentrated
on linseed oil, which I think gives the best result. Linseed oil
and linseed-oil paint are vast topics in themselves, but I hope
I offer you a starting point.

Linseed oil

I prefer to use oil on wood, rather than varnish or wax. Varnish is like adding a film on top of the wood. Wax gives a nice matte feeling, but it doesn't harden and is easily worn. However, oil sinks into the wood and lets you feel its surface and texture. Oil allows the wood to age with beauty and also develop a deep patina. I use linseed oil without exception.

Linseed oil is obtained from flax seed and will harden without any additives. This gives linseed oil clear advantages over other non-drying oils. Once it has dried, linseed oil stays in the wood, doesn't stain and actually makes the surface of the wood harder. It is also a natural product. When I tell some people that I use linseed oil on spoons, for example, they think the oil is toxic. Pure linseed oil is not toxic, but there can be additives in the oil that are. If the oil is only intended for waterproofing decks, etc., it may contain anti-mould agents and siccative. So always check the ingredients on the label first.

I use linseed oil on spoons and cups to stop them attracting dirt and soaking up too much water, and also to make them easier to wash. When the wood is not treated with anything, the pores are left wide open and soak up grease and liquid. I also think the patina is much nicer when the spoon is oiled. But a lot of whittlers prefer not to oil their wood at all.

Finishing with linseed oil

A common misunderstanding regarding the use of linseed oil is that you should soak the wood in the oil for days. But, if you do this, the wood will contain a lot of oil that never hardens and that is a waste, I think.

I prefer to brush or soak the wood well with oil. I use a raw, cold-pressed oil that doesn't contain additives. I leave the wood (of the spoons, cups, or whatever I'm oiling) to dry and then soak it in the oil for 20 minutes. I then wipe off any excess oil. You can repeat this procedure to saturate the surface of wood, but I prefer to let the first coat of oil harden before putting on any more oil. The wood will be dry after a few days. I like to use oils refined from substances that reduce the drying time (try www.kalmarsand.se). Otherwise, the drying time can be longer.

Linseed oil can be sun-thickened. This is a process that bleaches and thickens the oil. The drying is faster and it doesn't darken as much. It is, however, a long process that takes three to four months, which means that sun-thickened oil is more expensive.

Below

An old painted cupboard.

Making linseed-oil paint

Linseed-oil paint is made from linseed oil and a dry colour pigment. As with linseed oil itself, the quality of the paint is important if you are to get good results – in fact, it is probably even more so. By a quality paint I mean one that has a good covering power. The covering power depends on the pigment, but also on the characteristics of the paint.

An appropriate way to understand what makes for a good paint is to create your own. Making your own linseed-oil paint is very easy, but a lot of work. I started making my own paint because I wasn't getting the results I wanted with the paint I'd been using and discovered a dissertation by Kerstin Knutsdotter Lyckman called "Linseed Oil, Then and Now". I later came across paint colours that worked and were of a good quality, and so I made less of my own paint, as there is quite a lot of effort involved.

As I said, linseed-oil paint consists of two ingredients: linseed oil and dry pigment. You can make your own paint simply by mixing the two. However, you need to mix the ingredients well. You want the pigment grains to be as small as possible. This is why many retail colours fail. You also want the oil to be really saturated with pigment. The more pigment, the more meagre the paint. A meagre paint gives a matte finish and also dries better. A paint that has a lot of pigment also has better covering power.

Above

Mixing pigment and oil on a marble board. The muller is made from a natural stone.

Left

An old stone and muller for mixing paint.

1

Mix the paint on a stone or glass plate. You could also use a mortar, but this makes the process a little more laborious. I also like to use a muller made from natural stone and a palette knife. Pour a few tablespoons of the pigment onto the stone or plate (the amount needed will depend on how much paint you want to make). Create a small, volcano-shaped pile. Pour a few drops of linseed oil on top of the pigment. Mix the pigment and oil together with the palette knife. Gradually pour in more oil until you get a dry paste.

2

Take the muller and grind the paste on the stone or plate. After a while, the paste will start to get looser and runnier. You can then add more pigment to make the paste drier. The ideal consistency is when it feels as if you are kneading dough with the muller.

Continue grinding and adding pigment several times, if you wish. This process ensures that every single grain has its own coat of oil and that no grain of pigment is left "dry". It also ensures that the paint is saturated with pigment, and the more you work the paint, the more meagre it will get.

You now have a smooth paste. Mix this with some more oil in a can or jar until it has the paint characteristics you want. Remember that linseed-oil paint should not be too runny.

How to paint

Linseed-oil paint has its own characteristics and it is important to follow a few rules if you want to achieve good results.

- Paint it on thin! Old painters have a saying: "You should have more paint in the can when you are finished painting than when you started." That is why the paint shouldn't be too runny, but quite heavy. Use a thick paintbrush, which holds a lot of paint, and preferably one made from natural hair, as this will give a good resistance when you brush on the paint. When you apply the paint, don't put it on plentifully – almost rub it on with the brush.

- Let the paint dry/harden completely before you apply the next coat. If the first coat has not hardened properly, the result can be a patchy surface.

Useful tips

- I use oil that isn't so pure when I mix paint. But I never paint kitchen utensils and such like, because I don't want to mix any pigments, which are made from minerals, with food. So, instead, I opt for a quick-drying oil.

- If you use a good-quality paint and apply it very thinly, you don't have to dilute the paint with turpentine or other solvents, as is often suggested for first coats. All the coats can be painted with undiluted paint.

- Paint as many coats as necessary. I think two coats are usually sufficient.

- Wash the paintbrush with soap. Soap dissolves fat. Pour a tablespoon or so of soap into your hand or a jar. Work the soap into the brush with your fingers or by pushing the brush down so that the strands are spread apart and the soap penetrates the brush. Repeat until all of the paint has been removed.

- Linseed oil produces heat when it oxidizes. Paper and cloths soaked in linseed oil might ignite! Throw these in a fireproof or airtight container, soak them in water or burn them.

EPILOGUE: A NOTE ON SIMPLICITY

I am sometimes amazed at how it's the small and simple things that give some kind of meaning to your life. Once, as a heartbroken youth, I was sitting on top of Åre mountain, where you have northern Europe's greatest vertical drop for skiing. I thought to myself, very plainly, that if, once a year or so, I could just find myself in a place like that, snowboarding on a piece of untouched nature, I would be okay.

Whittling has been my main purpose for 20 years. Wood can never be fully exhausted. There is always something new to discover. Yet it is strikingly primitive. In its simplest form, you are dependent on a knife and a piece of wood. And I also feel gratitude, as well as amazement, because it is reassuring to know that it takes so little effort to find joy.

In the last few years there has been a growing interest in craft and handmade objects. Some people even say that the handmade approach is a revolution that will save the world. I don't think making things by hand will save the world, but in a way it can save one person: the one that picks up an object and finds something that brings a sense of simplicity, affinity and even inner peace to a complex everyday life.

I know an interior designer who, during an especially rough period in his life, sat down at the end of each day and watched a YouTube video of a clog-maker filmed in the early 1900s. The video had no sound and was quite long. But it gave him comfort.

I hope that you won't have to sit in front of a screen to feel the comfort you get from whittling, but that you will find it in actually having a piece of fresh wood in your hand and starting a journey that might last a lifetime. And I hope that I will see you sometime, in the fellowship of whittlers that is shaping a new culture of woodworking and whittling around the world. And, although it might seem like a long journey when you make your first few fumbly cuts, it is one that is always rewarding, often remarkable, and rarely dull.

RESOURCES

Below is a list of suppliers of the tools and materials that I like to use. There are lots more, but I know that these producers are reliable and dedicated to making really good products.

Tools

- MoraKniv
  Morakniv AB
  Box 407
  792 27 Mora
  Sweden
  www.morakniv.se
  (for a list of worldwide retailers or ordering online)

  Laminated carving knives (models 105, 106 and 120)

- Gränsfors Bruk
  Gränsfors 381
  820 70 Bergsjö
  Sweden
  www.gransforsbruk.com
  (for a list of worldwide retailers)

  Small and large carving hatchets, large carving axes, adzes and froes, plus general information on axes

- Klensmide
  www.klensmide.se
  (for a list of retailers or ordering online)

  Hans Karlsson tools, spoon knives, gouges, scorps and drawknives

- Pfeil
  www.pfeiltools.com
  (for a list of worldwide retailers)

  Chisels, straight and bent gouges, drawknives and sculpting tools

Linseed oil and paints

- Ottossonfarg
  Lillegårdsvägen 14
  247 70 Genarp
  Sweden

  info@ottossonfarg.com
  www.ottossonfarg.com
  (for a list of retailers)

  Linseed oil, linseed-oil paint, dry pigments and brushes, plus lots of information and how-to videos

INDEX

(page numbers in italic type refer to photographs and captions)

A

Acer platanoides (maple) 34, 64, 70, *71*, 97
adzes 21, 41, 93, 101, *101*, 157
alder (Alnus) 64, 70, 74
Almén, Torsten 35
Alnus (alder) 64, 70, 74
apple (Malus domestica) 20, 61, *71*
Åre 155
ash (Fraxinus excelsior) 70, *71*
aspen (Populus tremula) 69, 74
axe-smiths 23
axes 20, 21, *22*, 23, 36, 157
  author's recommendations 24
  broad *20*, 69
  safe use of, see safety

B

bench joinery 50
birch (Betula) 63, 67, 74, 79, *143*
  bark 9, 91, *130*, *131*, *132*, *134*, *135*, *136*, *137*, *139*, *140*, *141*
  boxes 8, 106, 126, 130, 133–41, *134–41*
  cups 6, *8*
  knives 6
  working with 133–41
breadboard *148*
burls 31, *62*, *89*
  cups made from 95
  crook, ladles 106
  root *130*, *137*, *138*
  spoons *13*, *97*
  troughs and bowls 66
blanks *40*, *41*, *42*, 66, 82, 94, 98–9, *98*, *99*, 101–3 passim, 109
  how to make 74, 76, 77, 78–9, *78*, *79*, 120
Blixt, Nils *128*, 130, 134, 137, 140
Bo Helgesson *19*, *27*, 31, *31*
boards, how to create 51–3, *51*, *52*, *53*
Bortom Åa 126, *127*, 129
box-making 8, 106, 126, 130,

133–41, *134–41*
breadboard 147, *147*, 148, *148*
Brita (hostel manager) 126
broad axes *20*, 69 (see also axes)
Bullersjön, Lake 6, *7*, 8
burls *31*, 41, *62*, 88, *89*, *91*
  carving from 88, *90*, 91–5, *91*
  root *62*

C

carpentry 6, 22, 64, 69, 70, 108
carving:
  from burls 88, 91–5, *91*
  decorative 144
    chip 148, *148*, *149*
    lines 145–7, *145*, *146*
  drinking cups 88, *90*, 91–5, *92*, *94*, *95*
  knives for 18, 33, 145, 157 (see also by type)
  spatulas 77–9, *79*, 80, 81–7, *81*, *82*, *83*, *84*, *86*, *87*
  spoons 96–106, *97*, *101*, *102*, *103*, *104*, *105*, *106*
  tips on 58
  types of wood for 70
ceramic whetstones 48, 49, *49*
chisels 28, 111, 141, 157
chopping block *40*, 42–3, *42–3*
clog-making 155
courses 8, *36*, *37*, 96, 126, 129, 130
cracking 66
crooked wood 96
cross-grain 66, 69, 70
crosscutting 78, 79, *79*, 98–9, *98*, *99*, 100, *100*, 101, *101*, 113, *113*, 122, *122*
cup-making 6, *8*, 88, *90*, 91–5, *92*, *94*, *95*

D

Dala horses 17, 18, 48, 96
Dalecarlia 33
diamond whetstones 45
Djärv, Svante, see Svante Djärv
drawknives 21, 23, 157
  author's recommendations 33
  history of 33

how to use 32
drying process 53, 66, 94–5, 151
duodji 6, *31*, 88

E

Eliasson, Ingalill 130
Eliasson, Janne 126
Eskilstuna *17*

F

Fågelsjö 36, *36*, *37*, 126, *128*, 129, *130*
Fatmomakke 8
finishing 150–4
Finland 126, 130
fly fishing *40*
foraging 63
Fraxinus excelsior (ash) 70, *71*
froes 75, 157

G

goat willow (Salix caprea) 70
Gotland 48
gouges 23, 26, *27*, *28*, 157
Gränsfors Bruk *20*, *22*, 23, *23*, 24, 34, 157
green wood 66
grinding stone 45, *46*, *48*
Grundsjö 6
guild carpentry 108
guksi 88, *90*, *90*

H

Hälsingland 23, 126
hammers 54, 119, 123, 136
hand planes, see planes
Hans Karlsson 23, 24, *27*, *28*, 31, *31*, 33, 35, 157
hardwoods 64, 66, 70, *71*, 79 (see also by type)
hatchets 24, 34, 157 (see also axes)
heartwood 93
Hellberg, J.A. *17*
horse, see shaving horse
HV-school, Stockholm 8

J

J.A. Hellberg *17*

Japanese whetstones *48, 49*
Järvsö 69, 126
Jemt-Olov 106
joinery 34, 50, 64, 69, 108, *109,*
110, 111–14, *112, 113, 114, 115*

K
Kaj Embretssen 23
Karlsson, Hans, *see* Hans Karlsson
Karlsson, Niklas *7, 31, 32, 40,* 44,
107, 156
courses undertaken by 8, 96,
126, 129, 130
early life of 6, 8, 36, 41
family members 6, 8, 9, 36, *40,*
62, 90
friends of *17,* 29, 41, 77, *91,* 106
Sami heritage 6, 8, 9 (*see also*
Sami culture)
kåsa 90
kata 8, 9
knives:
for carving, *see* carving
draw 21, 23, *32, 33, 157*
safe use of, *see* safety
spoon 29–30, *30,* 34
author's recommendations 31,
31
whittling 30, 36, 45
author's recommendations 17,
18
variety of *16, 17, 19*

L
ladles 106, *106,* 129
Lapland 6, 8
lime (*Tilia cordata*) 70
linseed oil 91, *109,* 148, 150, 151,
157
making paint with 152–3
Ljusnan, River *40*
lumberjacks 23

M
mallets 54, 75, *75,* 93, 111, 119, 136
Malus domestica (apple) *20,* 61, 71
maple (*Acer platanoides*) 34, 64,
70, *71,* 97
metal planes 55, *55* (*see also*
planes; wooden planes)
MoraKniv *17,* 18, *18,* 34, 157
moulding planes 115
Museum of Architecture 41

N
Nusnäs, wooden-horse carvers
of 17

O
old tools, care of *31*
Olsson, Stefan 77
Orsa 106
Öst, Per Nilsson 69, *69*

P
paint, how to make 152–3
painting 157
how to 154
peg racks 116, *116, 117*
how to make *118,* 119–20, *120,*
121, 122–3, *122, 123*
Pelle (uncle) *17*
Persson, Conny *19*
Persson, Ramon 6, 8
Pfeil *27, 28,* 33, 35, 157
pine (*Pinus sylvestris*) 64, *68,* 69,
69, 98, 119, 137, *137*
planes 50–5, *50, 51, 52,* 55
(*see also* metal planes;
wooden planes)
moulding 115
setting blade depth of 54
Populus tremula (aspen) 69, 74

R
reindeer herding 8–9
risk assessment 36
Rolf (uncle) 8, 9
Rönnqvist Töre *22, 23*
root burls *62*
rotting 66
rough wood, how to flatten 51–3,
51, 52, 53

S
S. Djärv Hantverk, *see* Svante Djärv
safety 36, 37, 85
Salix caprea (sallow/goat willow) 70
sallow (*Salix caprea*) *62,* 70
Sami culture 6, 8–9, *8, 9, 17, 31,*
34, 88, 90, *90, 94*
sanding, author's views on 12
scorps 23, 34, *34, 35,* 157
author's recommendations 35
self-sufficiency 63
shaving horse 33, 43, *43*
shelving 108, *109,* 115
how to make *110,* 111–14, *112, 113,*
114
simplicity 41
Skansen Museum 129
Slöjdkniv 18, *18*
smoothing plane 50, 51, 52, 111 (*see*
also planes)

softwoods 64, 70, *71* (*see also*
by type)
spoon carving 29–30, 96–106
making blanks, *see* blanks
spoon knives 29–30, *30,* 31, *31,*
34, 157
Stockholm 6, 8, 41, 96, 129
Sundelin, Magnus *31*
Sundqvist, Wille 23
Svante Djärv 23, *31,* 35
Sweden 6, 23, 33, 48, 66, 69,
130, 157

T
Tilia cordata (lime) 70
tool polishing 49
tool sharpening 45, *48,* 49, *49*
trees, *see* by type
try-squares 52

U
Undersvik *6, 7*
UNESCO 126
Upplands-Väsby 6

V
Viking Age *22*
Vindeln 8, 96

W
Wetterlings *20, 22, 23*
whetstones 36, 45, 46, 48, *48,*
49, 49
whittling *40*
courses 36, *37*
history of 33, 34
knives *16, 17, 18, 19,* 30, 36, 45
safety, *see* main entry
willow (*Salix*) 70
wood (*see also* trees by type):
carving, *see* main entry
grain 58
hard v. soft 70, *71*
how to split 21, 23, 42, 51–3
passim, 61, 64, 66, 69, 70,
74, 75–6, *75, 76, 77,* 98, *98,*
106, 108, 119, 136, 138, *138*
identifying 61
nails made from 137, *137*
sculpting *68, 69,* 157
types of 64 (*see also* main entries)
wooden planes 50, *51, 52,* 53–5, *55*
(*see also* metal planes; planes)